NEWSDESK LAW

A learning aid for journalism students in print, radio
and television and for citizen journalists who wish
to understand the legal disciplines of the trade.

All the case studies in Newsdesk Law are from
newspapers but the rules they explain apply in
precisely the same way to radio and television
productions.

Updates to the material in this book will be
carried online at: Newsdesk-UK.com

NEWSDESK LAW

Copyright 2010 by Vincent Kelly

First published 2010

Millstream Publications
12, Mill Street, Warwick, CV34 4HB
United Kingdom

ISBN: 978-0-9566049-0-3

Printed and bound in Great Britain by
CPI Antony Rowe, Chippenham and Eastbourne

CONTENTS

Libel

Contempt of Court

The Courts

The Courts (cont.)

Privacy

Freedom of Information

Copyright

Vincent Kelly LL.B is a former regional newspaper editor and a one-time British Campaigning Journalist of the Year. After leaving newspapers he taught Journalism and Media Law at the University of Central Lancashire and was a training consultant to the BBC and various newspaper groups.

"Good name in man and woman, dear my lord,
Is the immediate jewel of their souls:
Who steals my purse steals trash; 'tis something, nothing;
'Twas mine, 'tis his, and has been slave to thousands;
But he that filches from me my good name
Robs me of that which not enriches him

(Othello:Scene 3,Act 3)

Apologies for starting a law course with a quote from Shakespeare but the great man does make the point very well. The law of defamation is all about reputation. It exists to protect the good name of the McCanns and, importantly, it also exists to give protection to the media who correctly expose false reputations.

There are two ways in which you can damage a person's reputation. The most important for journalists is libel which is a defamatory statement in permanent form. Libel covers printed matter, TV and radio broadcasts, films and videos, the internet, right down to blogs, emails, even graffiti on a wall.

The second source of defamatory statements is transient and is known as slander. Slander is not really an important part of media law and is dealt with briefly at the back of this course.

A claim for libel consists of just a couple of A4 pages but when it drops on the editor's desk it can send shockwaves throughout the office. For some in the media - investigative reporters or gossip columnists or the proprietors of sensationalist newspapers – it's an occupational hazard but for most journalists it is bad, and unexpected, news.

One of the worst effects of a libel action is that it can have a chilling effect on campaigning and investigative journalism. Where once the mood was on the lines of publish-and-be-damned it now becomes kill-it-and-be-safe. It is important to understand that both of those extreme attitudes make for bad journalism.

To rush into print or to go on air without carefully considering the legal consequences is plain stupid. Worse, to kill a story because it might, just might, get you into trouble is a betrayal of the journalist's role as the public's watchdog.

If you have a clear understanding of the basic rules of libel you will become at once more careful and more courageous. And you will make sure you get your facts right.

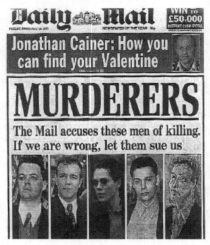

There are three elements which must be in place before a claimant wins a case for libel and we will use this extreme example to go through them. The first requirement is that you publish something defamatory, something that lowers a person's reputation in the eyes of reasonable people.

The classic legal test, using the Mail's page one as an example, is: Would being called Murderers.......

* Expose the five to hatred, ridicule or contempt or
* Cause them to be shunned or avoided or
* Would it tend to injure them in their trade or profession – in other words, in this case, stop them getting jobs?

The second requirement is that the defamatory words plainly apply to the claimant. That is obviously the case here but sometimes it's not so simple and the requirement gets detailed explanation later under the heading 'Identity'.

The third requirement is that the words complained of have been published to a third-party. Third-party means that someone other than the accuser (the Mail) and the accused (each of the five separately) has read the allegation. Just one third-party would do. The Mail's readership is in the millions.

The Mail's page one is an almost unique example of a newspaper savaging the reputations of five men in the most brutal way in the hope that they would sue for libel but knowing that they would not.

They accused the five of murdering the black teenager Stephen Lawrence who was stabbed to death in a racist attack in 1993. Three of the five, Gary Dobson, Neil Acourt and Luke Knight were accused in 1996 of murdering the 18-year-old.

The other two, Jamie Acourt and David Norris, were also widely believed to have been in the gang which attacked the student. But after various trials and legal procedures the five walked free and – at the time the Daily Mail page was published – could not be tried for the offence in a criminal court again.

BURDEN OF PROOF

In the criminal court the standard of proof required to convict them of murder was "beyond reasonable doubt." But libel (except in a few rare areas) is not a criminal offence. It is a civil matter where the standard of proof is the less rigorous "on the balance of probabilities."

The Daily Mail tried to get the five into a civil court by deliberately libelling them. If the five had sued, the Mail's lawyers would have been able to question them about the Stephen Lawrence murder under civil court rules and in the end invite the libel jury to conclude that it was at least probable that they had killed Stephen.

And, importantly for a libel trial, they would have been able to concentrate on the claimant's existing reputation and the reasons they had those reputations.

The Mail published this libel on St Valentine's Day 1997 and the five had one year before the limitation period for suing ran out. They never sued.

Now that we have republished the page the risk of a writ for libel arises again. This time on the author and publisher of these notes. And the one-year limitation period starts again each new day we allow people to access the page.

If the five had sued for libel, they would not then have to go on to prove that the Mail's accusation was false. The court would start off by presuming that it was false. It would be up to the Mail to prove – on the balance of probabilities – that the five, all of them, murdered Stephen Lawrence.

If the paper can prove the allegation 'Murderers' is true then it has the first of the seven defences to an action for libel - the defence of Justification. It is important right from the start to emphasise that when we plead Justification - "we are justified in printing this because it is true" - the burden of proof is on the paper. The Mail would have to demonstrate it was probable the five did murder Stephen Lawrence.

It is useful at this point to introduce some words of wisdom about the necessity of getting your facts right. Newspaper editor Matthew Lewin describes the day when, as a young journalist, he took a story to the renowned libel lawyer Peter Carter-Ruck.

" As we went through the piece, line by line and word by word," said Lewin, " the obstinate curtains impeding my understanding of the nature of allegation, defamation, supposition and real proof were finally lifted. I don't remember his exact words but they were something along the lines of:

" It matters not what you know or believe to be true,or feel certain must be true, or is obviously true or must - as a matter of sheer logic - be true. What matters is what you can actually show to be true Whenever you are unsure imagine yourself in the witness box in a case potentially involving many thousands of pounds in damages, under cross examination by a very sharp and very hostile barrister who barks at you: 'What proof do you have personally, Mr Lewin, **proof that you can actually show us,** to substantiate that allegation? ' "

Identity has to be established

Plainly you cannot damage someone's reputation if the people who read your defamatory words haven't a clue who you're writing about. In the case of the Daily Mail accusing five men of murder there is no doubt at all. Not only have they been named individually but their pictures have also been used to further identify them. But sometimes the media uses a defamatory story on the basis of "we're safe if we don't name them." The folly of this is demonstrated in the following story. Read through it and try to identify who has been libelled.

Leeds families were warned this week not to buy karate club memberships from doorstep salesmen.

These clubs are not registered with the sports governing body and so there are no checks on the standard of instruction nor on the instructors themselves.

Investigations are taking place in other UK cities after complaints about these clubs and the operation has now been reported in Leeds with residents in the south and west of the city receiving visits from these doorstep callers.

According to Mr Brian Porch,

general administrator of the English Karate Association, this is simply a "money making" operation.

"We have had lots of calls about this set-up. They are just taking people's money and then they disappear. The average person learning karate pays about £2 for a two-hour lesson. These people are charging £5 for one hour.

"Instructors are recruited from job centres or newspaper adverts and they then go round knocking on doors – particularly targeting homes with children.

"They are given basic karate

lessons, told to find a hall and then teach those who join.

"In contrast all our instructors are fully qualified, have first aid training and their backgrounds are checked to see if they have a criminal record."

Another problem was that they claimed to have full insurance cover but this was "very dubious", said Mr Porch.

Added Mr Porch: "These people are giving the sport a bad name. The UK are world karate champions and have a good reputation to maintain but they are just ripping people off."

GKR Karate - the people who sued the Leeds Weekly News - are not once mentioned in the story. Three points arise from this:

a. Even though no names were given, all GKR Karate had to demonstrate was that the story reasonably led people acquainted with the company to understand it referred to them.

Similarly, if you write a story about an individual without naming him all he has to demonstrate is that family or friends were able to recognise him from the story.

b. Actions for libel are not restricted to individuals. Corporations can also sue. A corporation is a set-up which has rights and responsibilities distinct from the people who form it. An incorporated company is a corporation formed for the purpose of carrying on a business. Think GKR Karate Inc. Think McDonalds Inc. – the Big Mac spent two years suing two campaigning vegans to protect its high-street trading reputation.

Other points: some associations are legally incorporated and can sue. Local authorities and central government cannot sue. Neither can political parties.

c. Group Defamation. The law allows groups of people, rather than individuals, to sue as a body but the courts keep the numbers as low as possible. For example: If you wrote "All lawyers are crooks" then plainly all the members of the legal profession could not sue because the reasonable man would know that many lawyers could not be crooks.

But when a former policeman alleged that he had been forced out of a police dog-handling team because of anti-semitism, all 12 members of the team sued as a group for libel and won.

So, in the case of GIVE 'EM THE CHOP, in addition to the company itself, all the canvassers for GKR Karate, provided they were few in number, might have sued as a group.

Main defences - an overview

The case histories used in this course are all from newspapers but the libel rules which apply to newspapers apply in precisely the same way to radio or television broadcasts or, indeed, to any publication which can be stored for reference – and that includes blogs and emails.

There are seven defences to defamation, four of which are essential learning for the working journalist. The four are:

JUSTIFICATION

FAIR COMMENT

STATUTORY PRIVILEGE

COMMON LAW PRIVILEGE.

The other three are:

Consent – an example of which is given later courtesy of George Galloway MP.

Offer of Amends – one for the lawyers to employ after a genuine mistake has resulted in a libel. Details in a separate chapter later.

Innocent dissemination – useful for chat shows and phone-ins where the broadcaster has no effective control over the maker of a defamatory statement. Again, details later.

A knowledge of how the Big Four defences work is essential. So is the awareness that defences might have to be combined to resist a libel claim. Each defence will be dealt with in detail later but, first, a brief overview of those four main defences starting with Justification and Fair Comment. There are two defamatory statements in the headlines on the Leeds Weekly News page one.

The first is a defamatory <u>fact</u>: "Doorstep salesmen flog dodgy karate lessons." The newspaper's defence here is Justification. The legal onus is on the Leeds Weekly News to prove that the karate lessons sold by the salesmen are 'dodgy'. GKR Karate do not have to prove anything. Right from the start the law takes the view that the 'dodgy lessons' allegation is false.

The second defamatory statement "GIVE 'EM THE CHOP" is not a fact to be protected by Justification it is advice to the paper's readers - <u>comment</u> based on the factual claim that the lessons are dodgy. The paper's defence to this is Fair Comment. But once again 'dodgy' has to be proved by the newspaper because comment can never be fair if it is presented on the back of inaccuracies.

*Lesson: If you cannot prove that what you have published is substantially true you have lost the defences of Justification and Fair Comment.. **Details of both defences later.***

This was how the Daily Mirror reported day one of the the libel case brought by MP Neil Hamilton against Mohamed al-Fayed over the claim by the owner of Harrods that he had paid Hamilton to ask questions for him in Parliament.

The headlines recording what George Carman QC, representing al-Fayed, said about Hamilton and what Hamilton's QC, Desmonde Brown, said about al-Fayed are savagely defamatory. If the lawyers had published those words outside the confines of the legal proceedings they would have left themselves open to writs for libel.

But legal proceedings are covered by Privilege. The defence of Privilege is an acknowledgement that on certain occasions it is necessary that a person be allowed to speak freely even if, when doing so, he falsely damages another person's reputation.

The occasions on which Privilege exist have been determined by Parliament. All these many privileged occasions are listed in the 1996 Defamation Act (a statute) and the protection granted to them is known as Statutory Privilege.

A second branch of Privilege, Common Law Privilege, has built up over the years by judicial precedents in the courts. Until comparatively recently Privilege, as far as the media was concerned, was confined to occasions which could be foreseen, like sessions of Parliament or court proceedings where the need for free speech is paramount. **Details later.**

Galloway was in Saddam's pay say secret Iraqi documents

Reynolds v Times Newspapers afforded the media the chance to gain Common Law Privilege for public interest stories about events, like that in the headlines above, which no one could possibly foresee. A public interest story provides information which the citizens of a democratic society are entitled to know - information in which citizens have a legitimate interest, not just a story which the public may find interesting.

This allegation that a British MP, a vehement critic of the Iraq war, had been in the pay of Saddam Hussein was of huge public interest. But was also hugely defamatory of George Galloway. The Daily Telegraph could not prove that the allegations were correct so could not employ the defence of Justification. When George Galloway sued, the Telegraph had to rely on Common Law Privilege, basically saying that while they could not prove the allegations it was their duty, in the public interest, to reveal them. **Details later.**

Words that spell danger

Currie wins libel award for paper's 'vilest lady' slur

There are key-words in every story, words that add colour, words that accuse, words that mock, and, most critical of all as far as libel is concerned, words that can be read two ways, one way by a journalist, the other way by a lawyer.

What follows is a perfect example of the danger of using words imprecisely.

It all began when the Express reported rumours that Currie was about to join the Labour Party to breath new life into her "clapped out" political career.

A columnist wrote that she would be no more acceptable to Labour than a "mass murderer", "a serial rapist", or "an active officer in Radovan Karadzic's death squad."

Currie's lawyer indicated that she was particularly upset by the headline which read
HOW EDWINA IS NOW THE VILEST LADY IN BRITAIN

This, he said, meant she was a nastier piece of work than even the notorious Myra Hindley and Rosemary West.

The Express accepted that the article went beyond the acceptable ambit of fair comment but claimed: "The article and headline in particular were not meant to be taken literally but were intended to be a strong piece of political comment."

Currie's lawyer argued that the words had to be taken literally and the jury agreed.

That careless use of words cost the Express substantial damages, believed to be £50,000, plus, of course, Currie's legal costs.

" I am very happy with it and have just spent some of it on a celebratory lunch," she said.

The reaction in the Express newsroom was not reported.

Next: How to weigh up words.

The journalist must learn to think of words as three-stage rockets.

STAGE ONE: The literal meaning. We have seen in the Currie story how important it is to be precise with words. We must be particularly careful when using slang expressions. See what happened when Radio City in Liverpool were sued for calling a local travel agent a 'con-man'.

In defence, the radio station said that when their reporter used the expression con-man he meant the agent had deceived "some at least of his customers". But the lawyers for the travel agent said the words con-man meant he was "habitually dishonest or cynical."

Radio City produced 19 former clients of the travel agent who all said they had had disappointing holidays. The travel agent produced 21 clients who said their holidays were fine. The jury preferred the lawyer's definition of con-man to that offered by the radio station. The use of the expression con-man cost Radio City £350,000 in damages plus big legal costs.

While we must be precise with our words, we must also be careful not to rely solely on proving the defamatory description was literally true. If you call a man a THIEF! in screaming headlines and his conviction was for stealing a packet of biscuits a couple of years ago you will be in trouble. The words have to be commensurate with the offence. LIAR! has to be a serial liar, a mega-liar, not a sometimes-fibber like you or me.

Beware, also, of raking up a long-buried past which may suggest that a stain on the person's character still exists. What is at stake is the person's reputation today. Not the reputation he has since lived down.

STAGE TWO: The inference (interpretation) a reasonable person would draw from the words.

TORY BOSS ARCHER PAYS OFF VICE GIRL.

This headline was literally true and the News of the World could prove Archer had paid £2, 000 to the prostitute. But they couldn't prove the *'pays off vice girl'* inference that Archer had paid her the money because he had had a sexual relationship with her. It cost the paper £50,000.

STAGE THREE: Innuendo (Latin for a nod and a wink).

The words may appear innocent on the surface but they become defamatory when read by people who are aware of certain additional facts or circumstances. For example, In 1986, a year after Lord Gowrie resigned as Minister for the Arts, the Star newspaper produced this paragraph.

A LORDLY PRICE TO PAY

" There's been much excited chatter as to why dashing, poetry-scribbling Minister Lord Gowrie left the Cabinet so suddenly. What expensive habits can he not support on an income of £33,000. I'm sure Gowrie himself would snort at suggestions that he was born with a silver spoon round his neck."

There are those among us who may see nothing wrong with that piece of social observation. There are others, more worldly-wise, who will recognise immediately that Lord Gowrie was being accused (wrongly) of being a cocaine user via the choice of words 'expensive habit', 'snort' and 'silver spoon'.

Defence of Justification

Justification is the easiest defence to understand. If you make a defamatory statement about someone but can prove it to be true you have the defence of Justification. Plain and simple.

But the courts will start with the presumption that what you wrote isn't true. It will be up to you to prove, on the balance of probabilities, that it is.

At the same time, Justification is certainly the most dangerous defence to employ when it comes to damages. An unsuccessful plea of justification could increase the damages because a libel jury is entitled to take into account in assessing the damages everything that takes place right up to the moment when they retire to consider the verdict.

They compensate the succeful plaintiff - not only for the actual defamation - but also for the insult to him caused by all the attendant publicity of the media arguing in court that what they wrote was correct.

There are a number of rules to remember about the defence.

 The plea of justification must be broad enough to cover every libellous imputation in the statement.

• Where the words complained of give rise to an inferential meaning as in the Archer Pays Off Vice Girl case it is not sufficient to prove they are literally true. You must also prove that the inference a reasonable person would draw from the fact is also true.

• Words must be read in the context in which they are used rather than in isolation. This can include everything else on the page. For example, a magazine quoted a story about the 'statuesque' opera singer Jessye Norman being trapped in a revolving door. She was advised to get out sideways and replied: "Honey, I ain't got no sideways."

Ms Norman sued and claimed that the quote conformed to a degrading racist stereotype of speaking in a vulgar way. The court, however, looked at the whole of the article and found it portrayed Ms Norman as a respected professional and a person of high standing. In that context the offending words could not be read as defamatory.

Cases like these are sometimes referred to as "bane and antidote". The bane is the potentially defamatory statement and the antidote the other words which take away the defamatory meaning. It is up to a libel jury to decide whether the antidote is sufficient to defeat the bane.

There are two guiding principles about libel in general and justification in particular.

1. Never treat a person's reputation lightly. If you have unearthed something to discredit a person be very sure of your facts. Most of these stories are about people who are in the public eye. They have spent years building a reputation and they are not going to let it go lightly. Legally – and morally – you have to be on the high ground.

2. People who give information to journalists nearly always have an angle. Mostly they want to damage the person they're tipping you off about or they want to spin a situation to their advantage. Some may be being paid for their information and may feel the need to exaggerate in order to justify the money.

So never expect to get the entire picture from that obliging informant. Try to get the other side's version also. Above all, never take a flier. It could turn out a nightmare.

"Cocky, fake, slimy, inelegant, ineloquent, charmless, witless, weird, sinister, glacially cold and luminescently remote, he may be the most chillingly repulsive politician of even this golden generation. If Pixar set out to create a CGI character to embody everything the public has learnt to despise about its political class, they'd be thrilled to come up with this lizardy schemer, who may have slipped through a tear in the fabric of space-time itself. Certainly he seems best suited to skulking beneath stone archways, in a purple robe, sibilantly sidling poison into the bloodstream of the medieval Vatican."

Picked out above is Matthew Norman's opinion of a Labour cabinet minister, written in the comment section of The Independent's during the build-up to the 2010 general election.

In style it follows closely the work of the Daily Mirror's star columnist Cassandra (William Connor) who, long, long ago, described the celebrity pianist Liberace as: "deadly, winking, sniggering, snuggling, chromium-plated, scent-impregnated, luminous, quivering, giggling, fruit-flavored, mincing,...... an ice-covered heap of mother love."

Cassandra pleaded fair comment when Liberace sued for libel but lost after the jury decided that 'fruit-flavoured' infered Liberace was homosexual, something which the pianist denied.

These two extreme examples are plainly "comment", part of the media package which includes parliamentary sketches, restaurant reviews, consumer articles, theatre crits, sports analysis, and scores of similar features.

But, with newspapers often beaten to the punch by radio and television so far as hard news and sport results is concerned, comment is increasingly inserted, sometimes unwittingly, into news stories as well. The headline Give Em The Chop, referred to earlier, is an example.

So all journalists, not only the writers of conventional comment pieces, need to be aware of the parameters of Fair Comment.

• Fair Comment defends opinions which by their nature cannot be factually true or false.

• It provides a defence for criticism of people in power or of people who place themselves in the public eye.

• An important element of the defence is that the writer presents all the facts upon which the comment is based so that the readers can make their own judgement of the issue.

Norman's "cocky, fake, slimy" was part of a 1,200 word piece which analysed the record of the cabinet minister. Cassandra's piece was based on Liberace's much-publicised television performances, so all his readers understood what he was talking about.

The Daily Mirror (next page) castigates a deputy prime minister in just one word. Decide for yourself whether it maintains the discipline required for the defence.

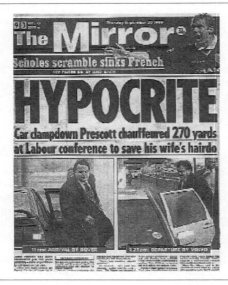

This is an extract from the Mirror story on the left:

John Prescott was twice chauffeured just 270 yards yesterday – as he urged Britain to cut down on car use........ Mr Prescott, asked by ITN why he took a car, snapped: "For security and because my wife does not like her hair blown about. Any other stupid questions?" Mr Prescott – who owns two Jaguars – earlier told the Labour conference: "The biggest environmental challenge we face is the poisoning of the earth's atmosphere."

Does the Mirror package qualify for the defence of fair comment? Do the headlines and the text above give the reader enough information to make their own judgements about Prescott's behaviour? Judge for yourself.

Fair comment must be

1. Based on fact
2. In good faith
3. Without malice
4. On a matter of public concern

BASED ON FACT

The important thing is that you must make sure your readers or viewers are sufficiently aware of the facts to judge for themselves how far your comment is justified. There are two ways of getting the facts across:

1. You may accurately report what a public person ('Car clampdown Prescott') has done ('chauffeured 270 yards at Labour conference to save his wife's hairdo') and then comment strongly: "Hypocrite" or

2. Without specifically reporting what the person has done identify the conduct with a reference the reader can understand. ' Watergate ', for instance, was a readily understood shorthand for the complicated issues which led to President Nixon's resignation and the scathing commentaries which followed.

IN GOOD FAITH

The Fair Comment defence will not succeed unless the jury is satisfied that the comment is one that an honest-minded person could make on the facts.

The one question that does not have to be answered is whether the comment is fair in the generally accepted sense of being reasonable, just or moderate.

The law was expressed by Lord Diplock: "People are entitled to hold and express strong views on matters of public interest, provided they are honestly held. They may be views which some or all of you think are exaggerated, obstinate or prejudiced. The basis of our public life is that the crank and the enthusiast can say what he honestly believes just as much as the reasonable man or woman."

The test therefore is: "Would any honest man, however prejudiced he may be, however exaggerated or obstinate his views, have said what this criticism has said? Is the comment relevant to the facts"?

The jury may think the comment is entirely wrong but if they are satisfied it is honest the defence will work. It is very hard to define what is 'honest.' It is far easier to demonstrate what is not honest and take the lesson from there.

One example was the judge's assessment of comments made in a libel case by the controversial historian David Irving. The judge said Irving's evidence was not honest. Rather it was..... "...motivated by a desire to present events in a manner consistent with his own ideological beliefs even if that involved distortion and manipulation of historical evidence."

3. AN ABSENCE OF MALICE

The leading judge Lord Nichols described malice in relation to Fair Comment thus: "Malice covers the case of a defendant who does not genuinely hold the view he expressed. In other words, when making the defamatory comment, the defendant acted dishonestly. He put forward something which, in truth, was not his view. It was a pretence. The law does not protect such statements."

4. MATTER OF PUBLIC CONCERN

The person about whom the newspaper is passing an opinion must be in the public arena – he/she could be a local councillor, a sports star, a government minister, a judge, a local chef, an author, a newspaper editor etc etc - anyone who has placed himself or herself in the public eye. Even then, the private conduct of such people is off-limits unless it has a bearing on their ability or qualifications for public office.

HOW NASTY CAN YOU GET?

We have seen that malice as far as Fair Comment is concerned is defined as writing something without honestly believing it to be true. There are also occasions when the comment is written out of sheer spite or ill-will.

Lord Nichols said in the Court of Appeal *(Cheng v Paul)* that spite or animosity, or intent to injure or whatever the motivation, of itself would not defeat the defence as long as the writer honestly believed in the opinion they wrote.

He added: "Critics need no longer be mealy mouthed in denouncing what they disagree with provided the objective limits of fair comment defence were established."

• The issue was one of public interest,
• The comment was readily recognisable as such and based on facts which   were probably true or protected by privilege,
• The article explicitly indicated what were the relevant facts and
• It was a comment which could have been made by an honest person, no matter how prejudiced or obstinate."

There are two grades of Statutory Privilege:

1. **Absolute Privilege** which gives immunity from an action for libel even if what was said was motivated by malice.

2. **Qualified Privilege** which provides the same immunity from an action for libel when reporting matters of public interest as long as certain conditions are met.

To understand the difference between the two consider what happened when Ian Paisley MP stood up in Parliament and read out a list of names belonging to people he said were responsible for 10 murders. This accusation was highly defamatory of those people. If privilege did not exist Paisley would be left with only the defence of Justification if he were sued.

But Paisley was protected by the Absolute Privilege which attaches to the proceedings of Parliament. This means that he could make defamatory statements even if the statements were made maliciously. Absolute Privilege is a complete answer and barrier to any action for defamation. It does not matter if the words are true or false.

The journalist in the Press Gallery who was reporting what Paisley said was also protected by privilege – but of a lesser kind. The reporter's privilege has strings attached, it is "qualified", and loses the protection of privilege if his report does not conform to four requirements.

Here are the five key paragraphs of the story and you will observe that the Telegraph did not publish the names which Paisley had read out earlier.

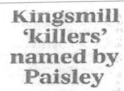

Kingsmill 'killers' named by Paisley

By Polly Newton
Political Staff

IAN Paisley last night used Parliamentary privilege to name the men allegedly responsible for killing 10 Protestants in Northern Ireland 23 years ago.
Mr Paisley said the IRA members behind the massacre

Ian Paisley last night used Parliamentary privilege to name the men allegedly responsible for killing 10 Protestants in Northern Ireland 23 years ago.

Mr Paisley said the IRA members behind the massacre at Kingsmill were named in a police dossier which made "interesting reading."

Mr Paisley went on to list a string of people he alleged were named in the dossier as being involved in Kingsmill killings.

A security source said last night that he recognised only one name, which he had heard Mr Paisley read out.

He added, however, that there was no evidence that the man had been involved in the Kingsmill massacre.

What to report of Paisley's speech presented the editor of the Telegraph with a dilemma. While Paisley,, protected by Absolute Privilege, was able to brand the men he named as murderers without any fear of being sued, the editor had to consider the four requirements governing Qualified Privilege before deciding what was safe to publish.

1. The report has to be fair and accurate.

This means it must be balanced, giving both sides of the issue in equal measure, and must be factually accurate. If, for instance, another MP had stood up after Paisley and said that what Paisley had alleged was incorrect then that would have had to be included. Equally there must be no significant factual errors in the story.

2. The report must be published without malice.

Malice in the context of Privilege has a different meaning from malice in the context of Fair Comment. Here it means ill-will or spite towards the claimant or any indirect or improper motive in the defendant's mind. The purpose of Qualified Privilege is to provide a protection when the provision of public interest information places the publisher at risk of being sued. If the publisher's dominant motive is not to perform this duty but rather to vent his spite or ill-will then he cannot use the defence. This would not affect the Telegraph but it might be relevant, for instance, if a publication set up to express violent sectarian views of Northern Ireland issues printed the names of the 10.

3. The report must be on a matter of public concern.

Plainly the Kingsmill massacre was a matter of public concern.

4. The publication of the report must be for the public benefit.

While compiling the story the Telegraph consulted a 'security source' who cast doubts on the allegations made by Paisley. This led to two sentences in the story:

"A security source said last night that he recognised only one name, which he had heard Mr Paisley read out. He added, however, that there was no evidence that the man had been involved in the Kingsmill massacre."

In addition to taking on board the doubts raised by the security expert, the Telegraph knew that it must be able to demonstrate that, if they printed the names, they printed them for the public benefit. It would not be for the public benefit, for instance, to print the names if there was a likelihood of reprisal killings. The Telegraph decided not to print the names.

✳ DOUBLE JEOPARDY

Notice that the Telegraph is keen to point out that the security expert they consulted "recognised only one name, which he had heard Mr Paisley read out."

This implied that the expert was present in the House at the time and actually heard Paisley first-hand. If the expert had not been there and the Telegraph reporter had instead read out the names to him later and said that Paisley had branded the 10 men murderers, then the reporter would have been passing on defamatory statements outside an occasion of privilege and this could have led to an action for slander. Details in 'Slander' later.

CATEGORY ONE- privileged without need to allow person defamed a right of reply

Fair and accurate reports of proceedings in public of:

A legislature anywhere in the world

A court anywhere in the world

A public inquiry by a government or legislature anywhere in the world

Proceedings anywhere in the world of an international organisation or an international conference.

Fair and accurate copies or extracts of written matter:

A copy or extract from any register or other document required by law to be open to public inspection.
A notice or advertisement published on the authority of a court, or of a judge or official of a court, anywhere in the world.
A copy or extract or extract from matter published on the authority of a government or legislature anywhere in the world.A copy or extract from matter published anywhere in the world by an international organisation or an international conference.

CATEGORY - privileged subject to a right of reply.

Written matter: A fair and accurate copy of or extract from a notice or other matter issued for the information of the public by:

A legislature in any member state of the European Union or the European Parliament

The government of any member state of the EU or any authority performing governmental functions in any member state or part of a member state or the European Commission.

('Governmental functions' embraces, for instance, an officer of state, chief officer of police, the head of a local authority)

An international organisation or international conference.

A court in any member state or the European Court of Justice or by a judge or officer of any such court.

Reports of the entire Proceedings of:

Any lawful public meeting. A public meeting is defined as a meeting, in good faith and lawfully held for lawful purposes and for the furtherance or discussion of any matter of public concern whether admission to the meeting is general or restricted. **A press conference, and any press releases issued, gets Privilege as a lawful public meeting.**

Any meeting of county council or district council committees or sub committees (not parish councils)

Magistrates acting otherwise than a court exercising judicial authority (e.g. a licensing bench)

Any commission, tribunal, committee or person conducting an inquiry authorised by an Act of Parliament, by the Crown or by a minister of the Crown.
A person authorised by a local authority to hold a local inquiry.

Any other tribunal, board, committee or body authorised by an Act of Parliament as long as the public and Press are not denied admission.

General meeting of any company or association constituted, registered or certified by or under an Act of Parliament or incorporated by Royal Charter - not being a private company as defined by the Companies Act 1948.

Limited protection: Reports of the <u>findings or decisions only</u> of any of the following associations, empowered by their constitutions to have control over members and to adjudicate on their conduct.

UK (or EU member state) association which promotes or encourages exercise in or interest in any: Art, Charity , Science, Religion, or Learning.

UK/ EU association which promotes or safeguards the interests of any: Trade, Business, Industry or Profession

UK/EU association which safeguards the interest of any Game, Sport, Pastime, to the playing of which members of the public are invited or admitted.

Statutory Privilege at work

This is a selection of newspaper cuttings which illustrate the way Statutory Privilege allows matters of public concern to be reported without fear of a claim for libel. The Amy Winehouse example, however, is also a cautionary tale.

Council meetings/Right of reply

LIVERPOOL'S council leader rejected claims that he is not fit to lead the city as the fall-out from the Mathew Street festival fiasco continued.

On a night when demands for an independent inquiry into the shambles were again knocked back, Lib Dem Cllr Warren Bradley insisted he would not "cave in".

He faced resignation calls from Labour opposition leader Joe Anderson who accused him of trying to hatch "a conspiracy" against Culture Company officials.

Cllr Anderson said: "Why should anyone now believe a single word the leader of this council says? We can only come to one conclusion from this tissue of lies, evasions and deceit.

"Unfit to lead, unfit to govern, unfit for office. A man who has proved through his actions and his words that he has no integrity, no honesty and no future."

The story is plainly damaging to Councillor Bradley's reputation. He is accused of conspiring against officials and being responsible for a tissue of lies, evasions and deceit. As ever, the protection of qualified privilege depends on the report being:

Fair and accurate

Without malice

On a matter of public interest and

Published for the public benefit.

Going through the story you will notice that there is no direct rebuttal of Anderson's sweeping indictment. All we have are Bradley's rejection of the claims and his insistence that he would not cave in. So the newsdesk would have to check that the story was fair. Did anyone stand up in council and deny the accusations in detail? If so they would have to be reported if the story was to qualify for statutory privilege.

The rest of the conditions seem more straightforward. The Echo would be unlikely to be malicious in its coverage and certainly the accusations were on a matter of public interest and printed for the benefit of the city's voters when election time comes around. .

Although local authorities cannot sue for libel, people within those authorities - councillors and officials - can sue as individuals. And privilege accorded to council meetings is in Category Two where a right of reply is accorded to anyone who thinks they have been libelled in a report of the proceedings. So Bradley would have that right to a reasonable explanation or contradiction of Anderson's attack, published in a suitable manner. This means in effect giving it something like the same show as the original story or, failing that, in a manner that is reasonable in the circumstances. For instance, if the original story was a page lead early in the paper, Bradley's reply should be placed on a similar page although not necessarily as a page lead. Buried among the ads at the back of the paper would not be sufficient.

Disciplinary panels

The protection of privilege is given to the findings or decisions of associations which have the power to discipline their members. They include, for examnple, the Law Society, the General Medical Council, the Football Association, the British Horse Racing Association and many more. It is important to remember that only the findings or decisions are covered by privilege – not the proceedings which led to those decisions.

Here is an example from the General Medical Council. I have not used the doctor's name but his local newspaper or broadcaster need have no such inhibitions and could in fact be said to have a duty to name him for the benefit of his potential patients.

The GMC's disciplinary panel decision was to impose conditions on Dr X's registration for a period of 18 months.They were:

1. Except in life-threatening emergencies, he must not undertake any consultations with female patients without a chaperone present. The chaperone must be a fully registered medical practitioner or fully registered nurse.

2. He must maintain a log detailing every case where he has undertaken a consultation with such a patient, which must be signed by the chaperone.

3. He must maintain a log detailing every case where he has undertaken a consultation with such a patient in a life-threatening emergency, without a chaperone present.

The inference here is that the doctor is not to be trusted to behave correctly with female patients, something plainly damaging to his reputation. If he was named by the local paper or radio station the editors would have to remember two points about qualified privilege:

1. Privilege would attach to the decision of the GMC only. If the story was embellished with details of the conduct which led to the order being imposed then those areas of the story would not be covered by privilege.

2. The doctor has the right of reply.

'Governmental' notices

Winehouse arrested by police

Singer Amy Winehouse has been released on bail after police arrested her in connection with an investigation into perverting the course of justice. Earlier, a Scotland Yard spokeswoman said: "A 24-year-old woman has been arrested by appointment at an east London police station."

The contents of notices issued for the information of the public by the government or any authority performing governmental functions are covered by privilege.'Governmental functions' includes local authorities and the police but does not include, for instance, NHS trusts, gas boards,

water boards etc because, while important, they are not performing the functions of government, they are not 'governing' anything.These governmental statements can be a great help because they are privileged but they also present a libel danger. An official statement by the Metropolitan Police is the backbone of the Winehouse story.

But note that the police do not put a name to the "24- year-old woman." The BBC goes beyond the protection of privilege to say that the woman was Amy Winehouse. If they are mistaken and the woman arrested was not Winehouse, then they have absolutely no protection at all if sued by the singer.

JUMPING TO CONCLUSIONS

Many libel cases start with journalists jumping to conclusions. This is the Telegraph story on the day after an IRA terrorist blew himself up when the bomb he was carrying detonated prematurely on a bus.

Another Irishman was lifted from the wreckage badly injured and rushed to hospital where he was placed in a small ward guarded by armed detectives.

The police gave the media those bare facts about the injured man. He was Irish, he was badly injured, he was being guarded by armed detectives.

If the media had stuck to those facts they would have been protected by privilege attaching to a police statement but newspapers drew their own conclusions and went further.

Many, like the Daily Telegraph, reported on the lines:

Bus bomber under gun guard
IRA man dies and accomplice injured

It turned out that the unfortunate Irishman in the small ward guarded by armed detectives was never the bus bomber's accomplice.

He had absolutely nothing at all to do with the bomber. He had been on his way to visit his mother. He was totally innocent and later sued a number of media outfits.

He was able easily to demonstrate that while he was not named in the reports, his family and friends knew he was the man the Telegraph and other papers alleged was a bus bomber. Having gone beyond the protection of privilege there was no libel defence left for the media.

Privilege in court reporting

A fair and accurate report, published contemporaneously, of court proceedings held in public attracts Absolute Privilege and is immune from an action for libel. There are occasions when a court report forfeits absolute privilege (because of the contemporaneous requirement) but is still protected by qualified privilege. What has to be remembered is that it is crucial to both types of privilege, Absolute and Qualified, that the court report is fair and accurate.

FAIR

The court report should be balanced, giving equal weight to both the prosecution and the defence. This does not mean giving equal space to both. At its simplest it means that you make sure to record the fact that the guilty man had pleaded not guilty, that you reported any mitigating points made on his behalf. There is a particular danger in reporting the prosecution's opening address and then leaving the case alone until a verdict is reached days, maybe weeks, later.

The Sunday Sport paid substantial damages to a police officer who had been cleared by the jury of indecent assault. The paper had reported the opening statement by the prosecution and the main evidence of the alleged victim but did not include her cross-examination by the defence which began the same day. During the cross-examination the alleged victim made a number of admissions which weakened the evidence she had given earlier and which the paper had reported. The Sunday Sport later briefly reported the policeman's acquittal. But they should also have reported the woman's admissions which effectively negated much of the adverse publicity the policeman had received.

ACCURATE

Allegations must not be confused with facts. The prosecution's opening statement in a trial, for instance, is not a recital of facts but of allegations which the jury will later decide are true or not. Above all ensure that all names, charges, pleas and verdicts are correct. As far as charges are concerned, it can be libellous to suggest that someone was convicted of a more serious charge than they actually were.

PUBLISHED CONTEMPORANEOUSLY

This means the next reasonably available edition of the paper or the next television or radio news bulletin. If the court report is not published contemporaneously it loses Absolute Privilege but is still protected by Qualified Privilege if all the conditions attaching to that defence are met.

How might this come about? Say the chairman of the council's road safety committee is arrested for drink driving and his case is heard when there is no reporter at the magistrates court to report his conviction. Some weeks later you hear that he has been banned from driving. You get the details of the case but you have lost absolute privilege because the report will not be contemporaneous with the case. What you still have left is qualified privilege with its requirements that his conviction was a matter of public interest and that publishing the report was for the public benefit.

Court documents

Documents seen by the judge or magistrates but not read in open court are not covered but there is qualified privilege for fair and accurate copies of, or extracts from, documents made available by the court.

We have seen that Parliament periodically reviews the 'public interest' occasions which it feels necessary to include in Defamation Acts as protected by qualified privilege - the statutory privilege list.

But there are other public interest issues which are just as important but which can never be anticipated and therefore cannot be protected by privilege in advance.

Some of these stories contain allegations which journalists are not able to prove but, following the House of Lords decision in Reynolds v Times Newspapers in 1999, can now be granted the protection of privilege. The one big proviso is that the journalism has to be of the highest standard.

Before Reynolds, investigative journalists had basically to rely on the defence of Justification when seeking to make allegations in the public interest.

Unless they were 100 per cent sure of their facts they laid themselves open to libel actions by public figures who would go to any lengths - including lying to the courts - to protect their supposed reputations and this had a distinctly chilling effect.

The Galloway story is a good example of a public interest story that came out of the blue in the immediate aftermath of the Iraq war.

Here we had a British MP, vehemently opposed to the Iraq war, supposedly being in the pay of Saddam Hussein. It was a story of huge public importance. But it was also hugely defamatory of George Galloway who promptly sued the paper for libel.

The Daily Telegraph did not have sufficient facts to run the defence of Justification and had to rely on the Reynolds defence.

The Reynolds defence is based on a checklist of 10 points which courts use to assess the quality and integrity of the journalism in order to establish whether it merits the protection of privilege.

The Telegraph lost the case and had to pay George Galloway damages and costs after being severely criticised by the court because of the way allegations were presented as matters of hard fact and because it did not give him sufficient opportunity to give his side of the affair.

On the next page we trace the origins of the Reynolds defence and go on to explain the 10-point legal checklist using the Galloway case as an example.

Mr Galloway has given permission for us to re-use this defamatory statement in order to illustrate the 'public interest' angle which has to be present if Common Law Privilege is run as a defence.

The Reynolds defence was the radical extension of a legal principle - common law privilege - which had existed for centuries. To understand the concept think of a character reference. The person who asks for it has a serious **interest** in finding out the truth about the person to whom he is about to offer a job.

The person who has to write the reference has a social **duty** to tell the truth about the applicant, warts and all. Social policy demands that a person who is asked to give a character reference must tell the truth.

STRICTLY CONFIDENTIAL

From: George Dutiful

To: Thomas Interested

I have known Donald Duckberry for about nine years and in my honest opinion, and I have no evidence to back this up, he is not to be trusted in any position in which he has access to the till. Signed: George Dutiful

In the above example George has a duty not to lie and, even though he had no proof, he clearly indicated that Donald was not to be trusted and the inference was that he was a thief. That is defamatory of Donald and George is therefore vulnerable to an action for libel because he has published the statement to a third party.

By his own admission he has no proof, so the defence of Justification is out. But English law has long protected the character reference with the defence of Privilege and if George writes the reference without malice he is safe.

If, however, George photocopied that reference and handed copies out on the street corner he would not get the protection of Privilege because, unlike Thomas Interested, the passers-by reading the reference had no legal interest in receiving it. They were not going to employ Duckberry so they did not need to know anything about his honesty or lack of it.

Common Law privilege, therefore, is based on the principle that a person who has a moral, legal or social duty to inform another person about a third party should be able to write freely without the fear of a writ for defamation hanging over every word.

Historically, the principle was difficult to extend to newspapers. First there was the issue of whether newspapers had a moral, legal or social duty to inform readers of matters of public concern.

Second, did each and every reader of the newspaper have a corresponding interest in receiving the information? Was the story of such concern to each individual reader that a wrongful allegation about a person whose life or conduct might never affect them should be protected by privilege?

The 1999 landmark decision of the House of Lords in Reynolds v Times Newspapers clarified the position. The Law Lords decided that, in certain circumstances:

* The media did have a **duty** to impart public interest information to its readers.

* There was certain information that the public at large had a legitimate **interest** in receiving.

For the first time, newspapers which previously had only the defence of justification when it came to attacking reputations, had a defence which did not rely solely on proving their allegations to be true. The Law Lords laid down the criteria by which a judge presiding over a libel trial would decide whether the story was protected by Common Law privilege.

The court will take into account the following 10 points before granting or withholding the defence of qualified privilege. We will use the Galloway case to illustrate them.

1. The seriousness of the allegation. The more serious the charge the more the public is misinformed and the individual harmed if the allegation is not true.

2. The nature of the information and the extent to which the subject matter was a matter of public concern.

   Bracket 1 and 2 together: This is an incredibly serious allegation to make against Galloway. If the newspaper is wrong the public will have been seriously misled and Galloway's reputation badly damaged. To balance that, the story is of real public interest because the MP has been a vehement critic of the war against Saddam.

3. The source of the information. Some informants have no direct knowledge of the events. Some have their own axes to grind or are being paid for their stories.

4. The steps taken to verify the information.

   Bracket 3 and 4 together: The Telegraph based its story on what it believed were genuine official documents unearthed after the defeat of Saddam. The authenticity of these documents are vital to its case. What steps did the Telegraph take to check they were genuine? During this process the judge will question the motives of anyone who provided the Telegraph with information that led to the discovery of the papers.

5. The status of the information. The allegation might already have been the subject of an investigation which commanded respect.

   This is not directly relevant to the Galloway case but in some cases the media makes allegations which they know can be backed up by the findings of, say, an official investigation which has hitherto been kept secret. Think leaks from politicians, civil servants, police officers.

6. The urgency of the matter. News was often a perishable commodity.

   This is the counterpoint to No 4, (the steps taken to verify the information). The law recognises that a story like the Galloway one is so big and so current – these were the first days of journalists getting access to what were purported to be Saddam's files – that the time might have been absolutely right to release it and that to delay for further checks would diminish its public interest impact.

7. Whether comment was sought from the plaintiff. He might have information others did not possess or had not disclosed. An approach to the plaintiff would not always be necessary.

8. Whether the article contained the gist of the plaintiff's side of the story.

   Bracket 7 and 8. Has the plaintiff been given a fair chance to put his side of the case? Often, especially when the information you get is sketchy, the plaintiff might be able to explain away the accusation. Equally, there are situations when to approach the subject of the story would be to tip them off in advance and enable them to take steps to frustrate a public interest story. After all that, was the plaintiff's side of the case presented in a fair, straightforward way?

9. The tone of the article. A newspaper could raise queries or call for an investigation. It need not adopt allegations as statements of fact.

   When the Telegraph lost its case the judge strongly criticized the coverage, including the newspaper's news reports, leaders, headlines and use of pictures, saying that the articles were not "neutral reportage" of the documents. The newspaper had not merely adopted the allegations in the documents but had "embraced them with relish and fervour".

10. The circumstances of the publication, including the timing.

This is a catch-all clause which would enable a libel judge to take into account other factors in the publication.

Lord Nichols, giving the leading judgment in Reynolds said a paper's unwillingness to reveal its sources should not be held against it when it claimed privilege.

"Above all," he said, " the court should have particular regard to the importance of freedom of expression. The press discharges vital functions as a bloodhound as well as a watchdog.The court should be slow to conclude that a publication was not in the public interest and therefore the public had no right to know, especially when the information is in the field of political discussion. Any lingering doubts should be resolved in favour of publication."

WRITING SAFE STORIES

Geraldine Proudler, a lawyer acting for the Guardian, analysed the way in which the courts had applied the Reynolds factors in early cases. Ms Proudler's conclusions:

1. The tone of the article is crucial - if the journalist represents serious allegations as being facts this will almost certainly cause a qualified privilege defence to fail.

2. It is very important to give the individual a proper opportunity to comment on the allegations and then report fully what he says - however far-fetched his explanation seems.

3. In a public interest case, qualified privilege can provide a defence when the journalist has got his facts wrong but ONLY when he properly applies the Reynolds factor.

Alastair Brett, the Legal Manager for Times Newspapers, provided a checklist for bringing a public interest story within the Reynolds criteria.

1. The subject matter was of genuine public interest or concern.

2. The paper had done its best to seek a response/comment from the person attacked in the piece.

3. The source of its information was honest, reliable and knowledgeable i.e. not driven by malice.

4. The paper had taken appropriate steps to verify the information and

5. It had adopted a suitable tone in the piece i.e. calling for a proper investigation rather than adopting what it has been told as gospel.

To sum up, the better the journalism, the more chance of getting the defence.

One story - four defences

This story was printed in the free-sheet Leeds Weekly News in August 1997 and the publishers were sued for Libel by GKR Karate (UK) Ltd. The publishers at first entered three defences - Justification, Fair Comment and Statutory Qualified Privilege. Then, shortly before the case started, the landmark judgement in the Reynolds case introduced a new form of Qualified Privilege. The Leeds Weekly News became the first newspaper to employ the new defence. We will use the story to go through the four main defences. First, though, as in any libel issue, you have first to isolate the defamatory statements in the story. The first two are in the headlines themselves, the rest are picked out in italics in the text.

1. GIVE ' EM THE CHOP

2. Doorstep salesmen flog dodgy karate lessons

LEEDS families were warned this week not to buy karate club memberships from doorstep salesmen.

These clubs are not registered with the sports governing body and *so there are no checks on the standard of instruction nor on the instructors themselves.(3)*

Investigations are taking place in other UK cities after complaints about these clubs and the operation has now been reported in Leeds with residents in the south and west of the city receiving visits from these doorstep callers.

According to Mr Brian Porch, general administrator of the English Karate Association, this is simply a money making operation.

"We have had lots of calls about this set-up. *They are just taking people's money and then they disappear. (4)*

"The average person learning karate pays about £2 for a two-hour lesson. These people are charging £5 for one hour.

"Instructors are recruited from job centres or newspaper adverts and they then go round knocking on doors – particularly targeting homes with children. They are given basic karate lessons, told to find a hall and then teach those who join. In contrast all our instructors are fully qualified, have first aid training and their backgrounds are checked to see if they have a criminal record."

Another problem was that they claimed to have full insurance cover but this was "very dubious." *(5)*

Ms Pauline Greer paid out £20 to cover registration and insurance for her 11-year-old daughter to join classes.

"I became suspicious when I couldn't get through to the telephone number they gave me.

"It was only when I spoke to a local karate instructor that I found they are not registered. If anything happened to my daughter I probably would not have any comeback.

"I want to warn others not to get involved. There are too many people in this area who can't afford to waste this kind of money ."

Added Mr Porch: "*These people are giving the sport a bad name. The UK are world karate champions and have a good reputation to maintain, but they are just ripping people off."* *(6)*

STAGE 2 – who is being libelled?

1. The 'dodgy' karate company was not named in the story but this did not matter. All GKR Karate had to demonstrate was that people who knew them could identify them from the piece. And it did not matter that GKR Karate was a corporation rather than an individual. Incorporated companies can sue for damage to their trading reputations.

2. Although it did not happen, any of the 'doorstep salesman' might have sued as individuals on the same basis of being identified by people who knew them. If their number was small enough they might have joined together and sued as a group.

STAGE 3 – who is being sued?

GKR Karate sued Brian Porch, plus the reporter who wrote the story and the paper itself. Note that all the allegations were made by Mr Porch not by the paper. This demonstrated the danger in the misguided belief " It's not us saying it. We're just reporting it so we're safe. " The paper, of course, had poured fuel on the defamatory fire with the headline GIVE 'EM THE CHOP.

STAGE 4 – Applying the defences of Justification and Fair Comment.

1. GIVE 'EM THE CHOP

The headline would "tend to injure the karate company in its trade" – that is the practical expression of one of the limbs of the test for libel. The headline is comment and is defended by Fair Comment. The requirements of that defence are:

The defamatory comment must be:

Based on fact, honest, without malice and on a matter of public interest.

2. Doorstep salesmen flog dodgy karate lessons

This is a statement of fact and the defence is Justification. The paper would have to prove the karate lessons were in fact 'dodgy'. This word brings up the danger of using imprecise slang.

3. " there are no checks on the standard of instruction nor on the instructors themselves".

Another two allegations that would have to be proved. This is an illustration of two important facts to remember:

1. Each defamatory statement must be considered within the context of the entire story.

2. Defamatory inferences may be drawn from statements which may seem fairly innocuous by themselves. Later in the story we read that Porch's instructors all have first-aid certificates and have all been checked for any criminal background. The inference is that GKR Karate's people would be helpless in an accident situation and possibly dangerous to children like Ms Greer's 11-year-old daughter.

Defence: Justification.

4. *"They are just taking people's money and then they disappear".*

Another statement combining two facts which would have to be proved by the paper – that the GKR salesmen received money and that they disappeared with no intention of returning.

Defence: Justification.

5. *Another problem was that they claimed to have full insurance cover but this was "very dubious"*

This is an example of the defamatory inference words can convey. The inference here is that the firm is lying.

Defence: Justiification.

6. *"These people are giving the sport a bad name. The UK are world karate champions and have a good reputation to maintain, but they are just ripping people off."*

There are elements of both defamatory comment "These people are giving the sport a bad name" which is defended by Fair Comment and defamatory fact "they are just ripping people off" defended by Justification.

STAGE 5 – Applying Statutory Qualified Privilege

In addition to the defences of Justification and Fair Comment the Leeds Weekly News at first claimed the protection of statutory qualified privilege for the story.

The basis of the defence was never outlined in court but it was likely based on the premise that Brian Porch was criticising GKR Karate in his official capacity of general administrator of the English Karate Association following an investigation into the company by the association.

The 1996 Defamation Act gives qualified privilege to reports of the findings or decisions of a UK association which promotes or safeguards the interest of any Game, Sport, Pastime, to the playing of which members of the public are invited or admitted.

If this were the basis of the defence the paper's lawyers would first have to demonstrate that Mr Porch's allegations were the findings of an investigation into GKR Karate by the association and not merely his own views.

The rules for statutory Qualified Privilege would than have had to be applied - and applied to each of the defendants individually:

1. Fair and accurate

Mr Porch's statement must be a fair and accurate account of the association's findings and the newspaper's report of Mr Porch's statement has to be fair and accurate.

2. Published without malice.

Malice would be established if it were shown that Mr Porch had no honest belief in the statement or was indifferent to its truth or falsity.

If Mr Porch had been malicious he himself would have lost the defence but his malice would not have transferred to the paper. Equally there was the possibility, discounted, that the reporter had no honest belief in the story or was indifferent to its truth or falsity.

3. On a matter of public concern.

If people were in fact being 'ripped off' it was plainly a matter of public concern.

4. For the public benefit.

The doorstep selling was supposedly taking place at the time of the paper's publication so it was a benefit for the public to be warned.

Next page: Stage 6 - Applying the Reynolds test

STAGE 6– Applying the Reynolds test.

The first and obvious requirement for the Reynolds defence is that the story is a "public interest" one. The Leeds Weekly News case was the first time the Reynolds rules had been applied and the judge decided to establish whether the paper was entitled to claim the defence <u>before</u> the jury heard the newspaper's other three defences.

This decision by the judge was crucial. If the newspaper was entitled to the Reynolds defence then the case ended right there. There would be no need for the paper to offer the original defences of justification, fair comment and statutory qualified privilege which they had to rely on before Reynolds.

This, in brief, is how the 10 points were tested:

1.The gravity of the allegation.

George Carman QC, the counsel for GKR Karate said the allegations were grave. The company was accused of a criminal offence, taking people's money and disappearing.

2. The extent to which the allegation was a matter of public concern.

Only a tiny minority of the 400,000 readers of the Leeds Weekly News could possibly be termed to have an interest in buying karate lessons. But the judge, Sir Oliver Popplewell, ruled:

"This was a publication to the world at large but limited, albeit to quite a substantial number, to those who lived in the area and to whom the issue of karate selling in the area would be of immediate concern. Did the public at Leeds have a legitimate interest in receiving the information and were the defendants under a social and moral duty to communicate to the public in Leeds the particular information contained in the article on this particular occasion?" The judge's answer: " Yes."

3. The source of the information – there were three sources.

• A reader who had handed over £20 to GKR to cover registration and insurance rang the paper to complain of her direct experience. The reader said she had spoken to a chief instructor at South Leeds Sports Centre who told her that GKR Karate were not registered, the people teaching had no qualifications, and GKR were charging £80 for four months training compared with £15 at South Leeds Sports Centre.

• The reporter received the same allegations from the instructor when she phoned him.

• The instructor also gave her the name of Brian Porch, general administrator of the English Karate Governing Body, whom she quoted extensively in the story.

4. The steps taken to check the information.

Carman QC alleged that the reporter made no adequate investigation before publication. He said that given the serious allegations in the article, which included allegations of dishonesty, the story fell far short of the standards of responsible journalism. The reporter did not see any of her three main sources and conducted her inquiries solely by telephone.

5. The status of the information

The judge said that though the reporter did not come face to face with either the reader who complained, the chief instructor at the sports centre or Mr Porch she was quite entitled to rely on the positions they held and the material they provided. But it would not have been enough to rely solely on the reader, nor probably on the instructor. Mr Porch, however, the karate association general administrator, was particularly well positioned to give information.

6. The urgency of the matter – was there any need to rush into print without taking time to check the story further?

The doorstep selling of karate lessons was still going at the time of publication so there was cause to warn the readers without delay.

7. Whether the company against whom the allegation was made was approached for a comment.

The reporter made one attempt to speak to GKR and left a message on a pager but Carman submitted the reporter did not give GKR a reasonable opportunity to respond. The judge agreed and said neglecting to do so went against the reporter.

8. Whether the story contained a gist of GKR's side of the story

The reporter had rung Leeds Trading Standards to inquire about GKR Karate and was told there had been no complaints about them. In the article the reporter failed to mention either the inquiry or the Trading Standards' reply. That omission was put it in the balance against the reporter.

9. The tone of the article

The headline writer essentially acted as judge and jury when going beyond a factual summary of the essence of the story.

10. The circumstances of publication.

There were no other factors to be considered under this catch-all section.

STAGE 7 - the judge's decision

Sir Oliver Popplewell, ruled that the article was covered by Common Law (Reynolds) Qualified Privilege. He said the reporter was an honest, sensible and responsible person on whose evidence he could rely and who was naturally concerned by the dangers, particularly to children, resulting from the organisation.

"I reject the view that she was indifferent either to accuracy or truth". The reporter had based her article "on what she believed, honestly believed, was reliable evidence.

"It is not necessary or relevant to determine whether the publication was true or not. The question is rather whether in all the circumstances the public was entitled to know the particular information without the publisher making further such inquiries.

Stage 8 - appeal fails

GKR later appealed against the judge's decision to deal first with the issue of whether the paper was entitled to the Reynolds defence.

They said that this relieved the Leeds Weekly News of providing evidence to prove their allegations were true which they would have to have done if the defence of Justification was dealt with first.

The Court of Appeal backed the judge. It said that it was more expedient to get the privilege issue out of the way first because the process of the defence of Justification might have taken weeks.

Offer of Amends

The "Offer of Amends" defence is used in cases where the publisher has simply made a mistake. The classic example is the case of Newstead v Daily Express.

The Express reported that Harold Newstead, a 30-year-old man from Camberwell, had been sent to prison for nine months for bigamy.

Unfortunately for the paper there was another Harold Newstead, who worked in Camberwell, and who was certainly not a bigamist. This second Harold Newstead successfully sued for libel on the basis that the story had been understood by others to refer to him.

The Offer of Amends defence was introduced in the Defamation Act 1996 to cover cases like this. But there are conditions attached. The defence can only be used where the publisher of the defamatory words can demonstrate:

1. That he did not know and had no reason to believe that the statement complained of referred to the claimant and

2. He did not know and had no reason to believe that the statement was false and defamatory of the claimant.

To get the defence the publisher has to make a written offer of a suitable correction and apology and pay the claimant suitable damages.

If the offer of amends is not accepted and the claimant decides to push ahead with a libel action the publisher will then have a defence to the action, provided that the court accepts that he did not know, and had no reason to believe, that the words complained of were false and defamatory of the claimant.

In the event of a libel action the onus is on the claimant to show that the publication was not innocent.

Innocent Dissemination

In most libel cases the people who get sued are the author of the offending articles, the editor of the publication and the publisher.

But there are many other links in the publishing chain who could also be sued should the claimant wish – printers, distributors, the sellers of the offending publication and the internet service providers that host websites.

The Innocent Dissemination defence was introduced in the 1996 Defamation Act to provide a defence for such people. The defence applies to anyone who:

1. was not the author, editor or publisher of the defamatory statement

2. took reasonable care in relation to its publication and

3. did not know or have reason to know that whatever part they played in the publication caused or contributed to the publication of a defamatory statement.

BROADCASTERS

Besides the people in the supply chain, the defence also covers broadcasters of live programmes like phone-ins or chat shows which encourage contributions from people over whose words the broadcaster has little control.

But the simple fact that the broadcaster has no immediate editorial control is not sufficient for the defence.

The defence demands that the broadcaster has taken reasonable care like, for instance, using a delay button which provides a sufficient time-span for defamatory words to be blocked.

'Live' coverage of the Chilcot Inquiry into the Iraq war was delayed for one minute by both BBC News and Sky News for this purpose among others.

It is also important to remember that the defence would not cover any gaffes perpetrated by broadcasters presiding over chat shows or phone-ins or by journalists conducting live to air interviews. The requirement of 'reasonable care' implies sufficient training to ensure they don't blurt out things they shouldn't.

Slander

The big difference between libel and slander is that libel is defamation in a permanent form and slander is defamation spoken and transient.

The other difference is that libel presumes that actual monetary damage has been done to the claimant. In slander actions the claimant has to prove actual monetary loss – except in four specific cases:

- Any imputation that an individual has committed a crime punishable by death or imprisonment.
- Any imputation that an individual is suffering from certain contagious or objectionable diseases.
- Any imputation of unchastity in a woman.
- Any statement calculated to disparage an individual in his office, profession, calling, trade or business.

The journalist investigating a story must always be careful of the danger of slander when he seeks information.

The Daily Telegraph story we used earlier to illustrate the difference between absolute privilege and statutory qualified privilege concerned Ian Paisley MP naming 10 men as having been involved in a massacre in Northern Ireland. We use it again to illustrate not only slander but also the fact that more than one media law issue can often be found in one story.

> Ian Paisley last night used Parliamentary privilege to name the men allegedly responsible for killing 10 Protestants in Northern Ireland 23 years ago.
>
> Mr Paisley said the IRA members behind the massacre at Kingsmill were named in a police dossier which made "interesting reading." He went on to list a string of people he alleged were named in the dossier as being involved in Kingsmill killings.
>
> A security source said last night that he recognised only one name, which he had heard Mr Paisley read out. He added, however, that there was no evidence that the man had been involved in the Kingsmill massacre.

Notice that the Telegraph is keen to point out that the security expert they consulted "recognised only one name, which he had heard Mr Paisley read out." This implied that the expert was present in the House at the time and actually heard Paisley first-hand. If the expert had not been there and the Telegraph reporter had instead read out the names to him later and said that Paisley had branded the 10 men murderers then the reporter would have been passing on defamatory statements outside an occasion of privilege.

This could have led to an action for slander without any of the 10 having to prove actual monetary damage because the imputation is that they had committed a crime punishable by death or imprisonment - one of the four categories listed above.

Libel rules to remember

To succeed in an action for libel the claimant must prove three things:

- The statement complained of was defamatory.
- The statement referred to the claimant
- The statement was published to a third-party.

Defamatory. A statement which exposes a person to: Hatred, ridicule or contempt or which causes him to be shunned or avoided or which has a tendency to injure him in his office, trade or profession in the estimation of right-thinking members of society generally.

Identity: "Are the words such as would reasonably lead persons acquainted with the plaintiff to believe that he was the person referred to ?"

DEFENCES

Consent - consent was given to the content of the article including any potentially defamatory allegations.

Justification —what you have written is substantially true.

Fair Comment —the comment is based on fact, is written in good faith, is without malice and is on a matter of public concern.

Absolute Statutory Privilege —the report is fair and accurate and published contemporaneously.

Qualified Statutory Privilege —the report is fair and accurate, without malice, on a matter of public interest and published for the public benefit.

Common Law Qualified Privilege (the 10-point Reynolds defence)

1. The seriousness of the allegation.
2. The extent to which it is of public concern.
3. Source of the information.
4. Steps taken to verify the information.
5. Status of the information.
6. Urgency of the matter.
7. Was comment sought from plaintiff ?
8. Did article contain gist of plaintiff's side of the story?
9. The tone of the article.
10. Circumstances of publication, including the timing.

Offer of amends - the publisher did not know, or have reason to believe, that the defamatory statement could be taken to refer to the claimant.

Innocent Dissemination - a defence for many of the parties in the publishing chain who are not the author, editor or publisher of the defamatory statement. They have, though, to take reasonable steps to prevent libels.

TWO FACES OF MALICE: In Fair Comment malice means making a defamatory comment without honestly believing it to be true or to being reckless as to whether it was true or not. Malice in the popularly understood form of spite or ill-will is allowable.

By contrast, in the case of Privilege, malice means ill-will or spite towards the claimant or any indirect or improper motive in the defendant's mind. The purpose of Qualified Privilege is to provide a protection when the provision of public interest information places the publisher at risk of being sued.

If the publisher's dominant motive is not to perform this public duty but rather to vent his spite or ill-will then he cannot use the defence.

CONTEMPT OF COURT

This section on Contempt of Court covers two areas of Media Law which should be considered together:

1. Contempt of Court rules as they affect crime reporting by the media.

2. Restrictions on the reporting of preliminary court proceedings prior to a person going on trial before a jury.

Both sets of rules are designed to ensure that a person accused of a serious crime gets a fair trial. This is how the judge at one of Britain's most emotive trials instructed the jury on how a fair trial is conducted.

Mr Justice Moses said Ian Huntley and Maxine Carr were innocent until proved guilty over the deaths of 10-year-olds Holly Wells and Jessica Chapman.

He told the jury of seven women and five men they should remain 'cool and calm' and try the pair on the evidence and not what they read about or saw on television.

He said: "The death of anyone, and perhaps especially children, gives rise to understandable concern and emotion but the courtroom – this courtroom – is not the place for any expression of emotion.

"It is the place where evidence is called and sifted and where cool and calm consideration of that evidence takes place uninfluenced by emotion, uninfluenced by sympathy.

"Only by your understanding and appreciation of that principle can a fair trial take place."

In his 15-minute speech the judge added: "The case concerns the deaths in Soham, Cambridgeshire, of two girls and it would be idle to pretend that you had not read about it or seen stories about it on television.

"So what is expected of you? What is required of each one of you sitting on the jury? It is this. You are required to be impartial. What does that mean?

"It means you try this case on the evidence you hear and see in this court uninfluenced and unprejudiced by anything you may have read, heard or seen elsewhere or anything you may in the future hear, read or see elsewhere.

"That is not evidence. It never becomes evidence. You and you alone are the judges of the facts as revealed by the evidence which will be called in this court."

He added: "That is what you are asked to do. I stress this because the essential duty of all of us....to do all that is humanly possible to ensure that this is a fair trial and a fair trial depends upon the impartiality of you, the jury.

"Impartiality also requires an open, unprejudiced mind. The defendants are innocent unless the prosecution, on the evidence, can make you sure of their guilt."

There are two main channels through which the jury's minds could be prejudiced. The most obvious is the blanket coverage by the media. The second is through the eventual jury reading or hearing reports of the preliminary court hearings prior to the full trial.

The media coverage is governed by the Contempt of Court Act 1981.

The court coverage is governed by the Magistrates Court Act 1980.

Judge blasts 'foolish' radio duo for Shipman contempt

A radio DJ was warned by the judge in the Shipman trial that he could have gone to jail for a "foolish" and "irresponsible" broadcast which might have led to a retrial.

Mark Kaye, drive time DJ on Preston radio station Rock FM and traffic girl Judith Vause were hauled into court by Mr Justice Forbes on the 38th day of the Shipman trial after Kaye declared on live radio that the defendant was "innocent until proved guilty as sin".

Vause was heard in the background shouting "guilty."

After listening to a tape of Kaye's show the judge told Kaye and Vause: "My preliminary view is that the broadcast was calculated to prejudice the fairness of this trial and that it was deliberate and the words themselves made it quite clear. And that, in my preliminary view is a blatant contempt of court."

Kaye and Vause escaped with that public dressing down.

The rules for contempt of court are laid out in the Contempt of Court Act 1981 which tells the media:

1. Precisely when the danger of contempt comes into operation. This is when the "initial step" has been taken, which means a person has been either:

Arrested or charged or a warrant has been issued for their arrest or a summons has been issued for them to appear in court.

2. How their stories will be assessed for contempt of court. The test is this:

Does the story create a substantial risk that the course of justice will be seriously impeded or prejudiced?

This is the process by which the court decides whether a story has created a substantial risk of serious prejudice in the mind of anyone who was later selected to serve on the jury hearing the case.

SUBSTANTIAL RISK: In effect this means simply: Would a potential juror actually have had the opportunity to read or hear the story in question? If the court was satisfied that the jury had not read or heard the story then there could be no prejudice and therefore no contempt. Plainly if the story was printed in a national newspaper or broadcast by a national radio station there is always going to be a substantial risk. But, say the prejudicial story was published in the Northern Echo in Darlington and the trial was held in Cornwall then there would be little chance of substantial risk because a potential juror, recruited from people living in Cornwall, could hardly be expected to have read it. Even here, though, it is best to be cautious because of the widespread impact of newspaper websites which are accessible all over the country. The best practice is to assume that the story will be read by a potential juror.

SERIOUS PREJUDICE: Once the 'substantial risk' test has been satisfied the assessment of whether the story would create serious prejudice in the minds of the jury then comes into play.

It does so first of all by determining how dramatic was the initial impact of the story. A screaming front page lead in the local paper would plainly have more impact on a potential juror than a down-page, three-par story on page 18 of a national.

Then there is the time gap. The longer the time between the story being published or broadcast and the jury retiring to reach its verdict, the less chance there is of the story being in contempt.

Newsdesks, therefore, should know the average time it takes in their Crown Court area for a case to go from arrest to trial. If the story is published on the night before the trial opens then the risk of contempt is obviously higher than if it were published six months previously - which is about the national average for a case to get from arrest to trial at the crown court.

The fade factor: Once the matters of dramatic coverage and time gaps are assessed the court would pay consideration to the fade factor.

The theory is that if a juror:

- listens in court to all the evidence presented by the prosecution and the defence,
- hears all the witnesses being cross-examined,
- and then is guided by the trial judge on what is, and is not, important,

then any initial prejudicial impact the story might have had six months previously will fade away as the juror concentrates on the actual evidence six months later.

But despite the time gap, despite the fade factor, there is a particular danger in revealing that the defendant has a previous conviction. A jury (which must presume that a defendant has an unblemished past) would find that hard to forget.

Intent: Contempt under the Contempt of Court Act is a strict liability offence. This means that the prosecution - unlike in most criminal cases - does not have to prove either wrongful intent or negligence in respect of the offence.

Trend: The trend is towards liberalisation when it comes to applying the Contempt of Court Act 1981. Judges seem to have accepted that most pre-trial coverage, while maybe prejudicial, falls short of being seriously prejudicial at the moment the jury retires to consider its verdict. See the next page for a real-life example.

WHEN THE RESTRICTIONS END

The Contempt of Court Act 1981 ceases to be active when :

- The arrested person is released without charge - except when released on police bail.
- No arrest is made within 12 months of the issue of the warrant
- The case is discontinued
- The defendant is acquitted or sentenced
- The defendant is found unfit to be tried, or unfit to plead or the court orders the charge to lie on the file.

Karen Matthews was branded unfit to be a mum yesterday – by her own SISTER.

Julie Poskitt, 37, claimed Karen forgot how many children she had, stuck plastic bags instead of nappies on her children's bottoms and even snubbed the funeral of her own Down's syndrome nephew.

Julie said: "When Shannon first went missing, Karen told everyone she had six children. It took her days to remember she had seven. I remember screaming at the telly because even though I'm not their mother I knew she had seven.

"That tells you everything you need to know about Karen as a mother. She must be unfit to be a parent because you don't forget do you? You just don't forget. Karen never bought nappies.I couldn't believe it. I was disgusted. What kind of a mum would do that?"

These two items from the Daily Mirror of April 8, 2008 are examples of the way many newspapers and broadcasters ignore contempt of court rules when they cover crime stories.

There is no doubt the dramatic page one is seriously prejudicial to Karen Matthews who was to appear in the crown court seven months later charged with kidnapping, false imprisonment and perverting the course of justice.

Matthews had been arrested – the 'initial step' - on April 6 so the Contempt of Court Act restrictions were in force when the Daily Mirror printed the picture and headline two days later. If the case did go to trial, the hearing would most likely be held at the crown court in nearby Leeds and the 12 people who would eventually sit on the jury would be drawn from the surrounding area. The Mirror is sold throughout that area and there was obviously a 'substantial risk' that a potential juror would have seen it.

The headline I KNEW WHERE SHE WAS had a direct bearing on the charge of perverting the course of justice. Inside the paper, the Mirror, in common with other newspapers, published the interview with Matthew's sister. This indictment of Matthews' character would certainly put her in a bad light with the jury, yet when the case finally got to the crown court there were no applications by the defence that a fair trial was impossible. Instead Matthews' barrister Frances Oldham QC told the jury her client had been "demonised" by the media.

She said: "The media has decided that Karen Matthews is guilty, the police have decided that Karen Matthews is guilty. It would be easy to approach Karen Matthews' evidence on the basis she's a liar. She has been demonised in the media and you could be forgiven for expecting the worst from her."

Ms Oldham added: "There are only 12 people in the whole of this country who have had the opportunity of considering, not just smear, not just injustice, not just prejudice, but evidence here, of evidence in this case."

The defence was, it seems, relying on the 'fade factor' - plus the jury's good sense - to reduce the media coverage to an irrelevance.

Matthews was found guilty on all three charges and later gaoled for eight years.

When it all goes wrong

This double-page spread led to:

1. An eight-week trial being abandoned at the cost of £8,000,000

2. A re-trial being ordered before a new jury,

3. The editor of the Sunday Mirror resigning.

4. The paper incurring a £75,000 fine and £54,000 costs.

5. Everyone involved having to go through the long-drawn out ordeal again.

The Leeds United players Lee Bowyer and Jonathan Woodgate and two friends had pleaded not guilty to affray and grievous bodily harm with intent regarding an attack on an Asian student, Sarfraz Najeib, who suffered serious injuries in an attack outside a Leeds nightclub.

After hearing eight weeks of evidence and after 21 hours of deliberation, the jury had still to return a verdict on the affray charges when the trial was abandoned the day after the feature was published in the Sunday Mirror.

The trial had originally been delayed by lengthy legal arguments from defence lawyers that their clients could not get a fair trial because the police had initially said they were investigating the attack as a racist incident. Although the crown prosecution service (CPS) had ruled out racism as a motive, the defence argued - in a session sitting without the jurors - that their clients' reputations had already been tarnished, Mr Justice Poole rejected these arguments but did go to great lengths to inform jurors that there was "absolutely no evidence of a racial motive" in the attack on Sarfraz.

On Sunday April 8, 2001, while the jury were having a break from their deliberations, the Sunday Mirror ran the interview with Sarfraz's father, Muhammad Najeib - despite a reporter having promised him that the article would not be used until the trial had finished.

Under the headline *I wish I had fled Britain when I was battered by racists*, Mr Najeib referred to a racist attack on himself and suggested that the assault on his son was also racially motivated. The next day several jurors admitted having seen the two-page interview,

Mr Justice Poole said such allegations made in a "mass circulation newspaper published yesterday within three days of the jury's retirement... carries with it a substantial risk of prejudice" and would make any verdict unsafe. The "highly emotive" interview had resurrected issues of racism. The trial was abandoned on April 9 and the retrial ordered for October – more than six months later.

Would the Sunday Mirror article prejudice the new jury or would the fade factor kick in again? The retrial lasted nine weeks. Woodgate was found guilty of affray and sentenced to 100 hours' community service. Bowyer was cleared of both charges.

Can a 'Monster' get a fair trial?

A fair trial? On the face of it definitely not. The page is packed with prejudice. Victor Farrant is exposed as a 'freed rapist', he is linked to a savage attack on an escort girl.

The police label him a dangerous man. The Sun labels him a MONSTER.

This Page One splash would plainly create a substantial risk of serious prejudice especially as the story reveals Farrant's past convictions.

But The Sun and the rest of the media are safe when they use police appeals for help in tracing a wanted man for whom a warrant has been issued even though there is every chance it could prejudice a jury.

What happens in real life is this: The page is plainly prejudicial in the worst possible way, that is in revealing past convictions but the Attorney General will not prosecute for contempt because the page is published in the interests of public safety – and the safety of the public in a case like this outweighs the fugitive's right to a fair trial.

As soon as Farrant was arrested – he was picked up five months later in the south of France after a tip-off from a hitchhiker who had seen his picture in the English press - the immunity from contempt of court proceedings ceased abruptly. Newspapers from then on should not have mentioned anything about his convictions for rape and GBH.

Despite the vilifying headlines Farrant went ahead and pleaded not guilty at the subsequent trial at Winchester Crown Court but the jury found him guilty on both counts and he was sentenced to life for murdering the divorcee and 18 years for the attempted murder of the escort girl.

The judge told him: "This murder was so terrible and you are so dangerous that in your case the sentence of life should mean just that.

After the trial Farrant's family issued a statement saying they hoped he would never again be free to inflict his "evil, savage deeds" on anyone.

A Crown Court trial takes place in front of a jury of 12 citizens who are charged with reaching a verdict solely on the evidence presented to them in court. If the jury was influenced by anything other than the courtroom evidence then that would be unfair.

There are two channels through which a jury might get prejudicial information either for or against the accused. As we have seen, one is through the media publishing sensational stories and backgrounders.

The other is through reports in the media of the various legal stages an accused must go through before he gets to plead not guilty at the crown court. The rules restricting what can be reported of the committal proceedings on the way to the trial at the crown court are contained in the **MAGISTRATES COURT ACT 1980**.

The provisions of this Act are designed to allow the case to be reported – justice must not only be done, it must be seen by the public to be done – but reported in such a way as to avoid prejudicing the all-important future jury trial. S8 of the Act limits the report of the committal to 10 factual points:

1. The name of the court and the names of the magistrates.

2. Names, addresses and occupations of parties and witnesses and the age of accused(s) and witnesses.

3. The offences with which the accused is charged, or a summary of them.

4. The names of barristers and solicitors in the case.

5. The decision of the court to commit the accused, or any of the accused for trial and any decisions on the disposal of the case of any accused not committed.

6. The charges on which the accused was committed, or a summary of them, and the court to which he was committed.

7. Where proceedings are adjourned the date and place to which they are adjourned.

8. Any arrangement as to bail.

9. Whether legal aid was granted.

10. Any decision of the examining magistrates to lift or not to lift the above reporting restrictions (1-9).

Reporting restrictions can be lifted if:

1. The accused applies to have them lifted. If so they must be lifted.

2. In a case involving more than one defendant the magistrates decide to commit none of the accused for trial.

3. The magistrates decide to try one or more of the accused summarily.

The Act allows the report to contain an account of any proceedings that took place before the decision to lift the restrictions was made.

If some accused are tried summarily and some are committed in the same proceedings the evidence relevant to those who have been tried summarily may be reported even if it impinges on the case of those sent for trial.

If an accused is committed for sentence there are no restrictions on the report because he has been tried summarily.

4. All the accused eventually have been tried at crown court. This means that evidence given at the committal, weeks earlier, can now be reported without waiting for any appeal. This delayed report of the committal proceedings, provided it is fair and accurate, will be treated as a contemporaneous report and will be protected.

It may be that in a case where there are two defendants one may want reporting restrictions lifted and his co-accused may not. If so, the examining magistrate may lift the restrictions only if he is satisfied that in the interests of justice it is right to do so.

S8 and the media

Sometimes the media go beyond the 10 pieces of information allowed when reporting restrictions are imposed. For example when the accused chooses jury trial for reasons unconnected with the seriousness of the charge or his previous record. It may be a matter of principle. Newspapers have reported this to be fair to the accused. The same is true when people complain of police treatment during questioning.

Granting bail

There is also the question of whether the accused should get bail while he waits for the trial to start: The rules governing bail applications are contained in: the Bail Act 1976. Under the Act magistrates are required to remand the accused on bail unless they are satisfied that there are substantial grounds for believing he will:

Abscond, commit other offences or interfere with the course of justice.
or
He should be kept in custody for his own safety or he is already serving a prison sentence.
or
There is not sufficient information available to make a decision.

Magistrates cannot grant bail to a person accused of homicide or rape if he has previously been convicted of such an offence. The magistrates must give their reasons for refusing bail or state their reasons for granting bail in the case of murder, manslaughter or rape. If bail is refused by magistrates the accused may apply to a judge in chambers.

Reporting applications for bail

S8 of the Magistrates Court Act restricts what may be reported to "arrangements as to bail on committal or adjournment." This means the amount of any surety, any requirements to report to the police, the surrender of passport or any warning not to interfere with witnesses etc. But the actual arguments as to whether bail should be granted cannot be published. Nor can the reasons for refusing bail which magistrates must give under the Bail Act 1976.

Working rule

The report should in no circumstances mention previous convictions or any other information that carries a serious risk of prejudicing the subsequent jury trial.

S4 Contempt of Court Act 1981

The Magistrates Court Act and the Bail Act deal with situations where it is known that the defendant is going for trial to the Crown Court. But there are other court reports which might also affect a jury trial.

PREVIOUS REPORTS

Imagine for a moment that you live in a small town which also contains a man who is constantly in trouble with the police. The numerous court cases in which he has been involved have all been recorded in your newspaper.

All your readers know that this man has convictions for minor violence. Now he has been charged with robbery with violence, a triable by indictment offence, and must go to the crown court for trial.

You limit your report of the sending for trial to the 10 factual points allowed by S8 of the Magistrates Courts Act 1980. But still, because of all the court reports in your paper about him, people who may be on the jury when he comes for trial cannot help but know that he has got previous, that most lingering of all prejudicial information.

So is your newspaper responsible for contempt of court for, over a period of time, informing a potential juror that our violent friend has previous convictions for violence? The answer is No. S4(1) of the Contempt of Court Act 1981 gives immunity from contempt proceedings provided the court reports the newspaper published were:

Fair and accurate and published contemporaneously, which means the first available edition (or programme if you are radio or television).

A real life example is that of the serial killers Fred and Rosemary West who together sexually assaulted and then murdered 10 young women. Fred West hanged himself while on remand in prison. Rosemary West pleaded not guilty to the 10 murders but was found guilty at Winchester Crown Court and sentenced to life imprisonment.

Earlier, when both were brought before Gloucester magistrates court and sent for trial at the crown court all that could be reported were the 10 points in S8 of the Magistrates Court Act 1980.

As we have noted, one of the gravest prejudices that can be planted in the mind of a juror is the fact that the accused has a previous conviction for the same offence or some similar offence.

Years before, the local Gloucestershire Echo had reported a court case in which the couple were convicted for sexually assaulting a 17-year-old girl.

The Gloucestershire Echo was perfectly entitled to report the sexual assault case when it happened (contemporaneously) but, and this is the crux of it, if they had dug out the cutting of the court report and used it again before the murder trial they would be in contempt of court for revealing that conviction and would have no defence because they would not be using the report contemporaneously. So the Gloucestershire Echo and other journalists in the know had to sit on that intriguing piece of information until Rose West's murder trial was over.

HIERARCHY OF COURTS

The rules of the Contempt of Court Act 1981 are far reaching. The Act's coverage extends far beyond the criminal courts. It applies, for instance, to various tribunals, to coroner's courts, to mental health review tribunals which decide on the freedom of people in mental institutions and many more. In practice, there is a hierarchy of courts and on the top of the pile is the Crown Court where major criminal trials are held and the liberty of the individual is at stake. A report from any of these lower courts could prejudice a crown court case.

Let us imagine the case of an inquest into the death of people who died when a mini-coach crashed on a motorway. One of the survivors gives evidence at the inquest which indicates that the driver had been joking and looking back at the passengers when the crash took place.

Mainly as a result of this evidence the inquest jury returns a verdict of unlawful killing in respect of the dead passengers, a verdict which was widely reported.Then, later, the driver is charged with the criminal offence of causing death by dangerous driving and has to answer the charge at the crown court.

The media which printed the damning inquest report would not be guilty of contempt if it followed the requirements of S4(1) - a fair and accurate report of the inquest, published contemporaneously.

POWER TO POSTPONE
S4(2) Contempt of Court Act 1981

If, while the inquest jury was actually considering its (subsequent unlawful killing) verdict, the coroner heard that the driver was to be prosecuted he could immediately take steps to avoid any prejudice to the crown court trial.

The coroner would be able to take advantage of another section of the Contempt of Court Act, S4(2), which allows him to order that the report of the inquest be postponed to avoid a substantial risk of serious prejudice at the crown court trial.

Before imposing a S4(2) order, the coroner would have to balance the risk of prejudice against the public's right to open justice. Broadly, the coroner would have to assess how substantial would be the risk of serious prejudice.

If he did impose a S4(2) order the media would still be able to publish the inquest verdict and evidence after the crown court case had been completed.

Section 5 of the Contempt of Court Act gives protection to stories which are a discussion of public affairs - as long as the risk of prejudice to a particular case is merely incidental to the wider discussion. The S5 defence could be said to be the legal fall-out of the Thalidomide campaign by the Sunday Times in the 1970s.

Note the headline: It is not the usual "The story they *couldn't suppress.*" It was the story they *actually suppressed* – and suppressed for four years. The 'they' were the House of Lords, then the country's top court.

The story was written as part of a campaign the Sunday Times was conducting on behalf of the victims of thalidomide who were suing the makers Distillers for damages.

The Sunday Times investigation revealed a number of factors which undermined the Distillers defence and the paper claimed that it was in the public interest for the article to be published.

But the House of Lords ruled that the article, if published, would be in contempt. The law lords said that the public interest in the proper administration of justice (only the evidence produced in court etc) outweighed the public interest in people being able to discuss the matters raised in the article.

Four years later, however, the European Court of Human Rights held that the House of Lords ruling violated article 10 of the European Human Rights Convention which protects freedom of expression.

The Sunday Times, therefore was able to go ahead and publish its investigation And the European court's ruling led to the new S5 defence being incorporated into the Contempt of Court Act 1981.

Publication made as or as part of a discussion in good faith of public affairs became permissible if the risk of impediment or prejudice to a particular legal proceedings was merely incidental to the discussion.

HOW DO YOU JUDGE 'INCIDENTAL'?

Look at the subject matter of the article and see how closely it related to the particular court case or legal action. The closer it relates to the particular facts of the case the greater the risk of it not being 'merely incidental' to the discussion.

If a local paper, for instance, did a critical backgrounder on hospital cleanliness in the NHS just at the time when the local hospital was being sued by a patient who picked up the MRSA bug that might be considered 'not merely incidental'.

'Helping the police with their inquiries'

This much-used phrase is convenient for the media but has no basis in law. There are two dangers inherent in the time from when a person starts 'helping the police with their inquiries' to the time when he is either charged or released.

Danger No 1

Proceedings may have become active and therefore liability for contempt of court may have started.

Section 3 of the Contempt of Court Act gives an editor a defence if, at the time of publication, having taken all reasonable care, he did not know, and had no reason to suspect, that proceedings in the particular case were active.

A newspaper, for instance, might be preparing to use a prejudicial story while a person was being interviewed by the police and the contempt of court rules did not apply. Then the police decide to charge the person and everything changes. The initial step, charging the person, has been taken and contempt of court rules immediately kick in.

If the presses were already running and it was too late to "pull" the prejudicial story the newspaper might be charged with contempt of court.

In a case like this – to claim the S3 defence - the editor would have to demonstrate that inquiries were being made of the police about the person's status right up to the time the paper went to press.

Danger No 2

If you name the man and he is later released without being charged he may sue for libel, claiming the phrase imputes guilt. The Defamation Acts, however, give qualified privilege to information issued on behalf of a chief officer of police - so if a newspaper does name a person who is being questioned it is best to do so on the back of an official statement if it can be obtained.

Common Law Contempt

As we have seen, the risk of contempt under the 1981 Act starts only when the 'initial step' is taken - a person is arrested or charged, or has a warrant or summons issued against him.

Common Law contempt covers the time before that initial step is taken but when a trial could plainly be seen to be imminent or pending.

If a known criminal, for instance, takes a group of people hostage and a newspaper identifies him and his previous convictions before he is arrested or charged or a warrant is issued then there is plainly going to be a risk of contempt to proceedings which will almost certainly take place.

There is one major difference with the Contempt of Court Act 1981. If the newspaper is prosecuted under Common Law contempt the prosecution has to prove that the editor intended to create prejudice.

The court can infer intent by taking account of all of the circumstances leading to publication.

This need for the crown to prove intent to prejudice does not apply to cases prosecuted under the Contempt of Court Act which is a strict liability code.

Common Law contempt can also be used against articles prejudicial to the course of justice *generally,* as distinct from the *particular* case governed by the 1981 Act.

THE COURTS

There she stands, Justice on top of the Old Bailey. In her right hand the sword of truth. In her left hand, carefully balanced, the scales of justice. Contrary to popular belief there is no blindfold. Justice is meant to have an unblinking stance in the face of political pressure or popular clamour.

There are two groups of courts which seek to dispense justice. Criminal courts deal with offences against society. Civil courts resolve disputes between individuals or companies, mostly over money. The justice they dispense is based on two codes, the Common Law and Statutory Law. Common Law evolved over centuries and began with kings imposing laws that applied to everyone in common. These basic laws then began to be interpreted by the king's judges in the light of differing circumstances. " You shall not kill." " Yes, but what if I killed while defending myself?"

The judges' decisions refined the basic rules. The reasonings which led to their decisions - known as precedents - became the building blocks of the common law. Today's judges refer to old precedents when they interpret the law to fit a new circumstance, in effect adding more building blocks to the law. Justice has to be consistent as well as fair.

Statutory Law, on the other hand, is created by the people through their representatives in Parliament. It is a constantly changing process that refines the law to fit in with the social conditions and debates of the time.

Right now the debates are on diverse subjects like anti-terrorist legislation, drugs control, the pirating of music from the internet, anti-social behaviour, car crime and all the other 'Law and Order' topics that journalists spend so much time writing about.

Media law can be studied either as a lot of fragmentary facts that you need to pass exams or by seeking to understand the big picture: why the rules are there and how they work in real life. What follows contains the basic rules for reporting the criminal and civil courts and also attempts to shine a tiny beam of light on the bigger picture.

Arrest and detain

This picture of a suffragette being arrested was taken nearly 100 years ago but it illustrates a fact of life which still obtains today. You can lawfully be deprived of your liberty – by force if necessary - and can be taken away into custody for a period specified by law without being charged and brought before a court.

The state's powers to deprive a person of his liberty by arresting him and holding him in police custody is of fundamental importance and before we consider the mechanics of court reporting we must first understand how people get to court in the first place.

Until a few years ago, if you were caught committing a minor offence a policeman would simply take your name and address and warn you that you were to be reported for the offence. And soon afterwards you would receive a Summons ordering you to attend the magistrates court at a certain time and date to answer for your sins.

But if you were caught assaulting someone, or shoplifting or driving while drunk it is odds-on that you will be arrested – that is deprived of your liberty – and, despite your protests, dragged if necessary to the police station and kept there against your will.

The purpose of the arrest is to compel an alleged wrongdoer's appearance to answer a criminal charge in a court of law. To deprive a person of his liberty is a big issue in a libertarian society and an unlawful or wrongful arrest amounts to false imprisonment and the authorities have to answer for it.

Until January 1, 2006, offences for which you could be arrested were confined to those for which the penalty, on first conviction, could be at least 5 years imprisonment. In addition, for obvious reasons, some offences like taking a car without authority or drunken driving were arrestable even though the maximum penalty was less than five years.

As stated, in a minor case an arrest was unnecessary. The alleged offender could – and still can - be summonsed by post to attend court. But, starting in January 2006, the Police and Criminal Evidence Act 1984 (PACE) was amended to give the police powers of arrest for all offences, no matter how trivial, petty or minor, which did not previously carry a power of arrest. This was the biggest expansion in decades of police powers to deprive people of their liberty. Officers now have the discretion to detain someone if they suspect any offence and think that an arrest is "necessary".

The new power of arrest can only be used where: " A constable has reasonable grounds for suspecting that you have committed or are attempting to commit an offence and it appears to the constable that service of a summons is impracticable or inappropriate." That is:
 • The police are not satisfied that the name and address you give for the service of a summons are correct or
  • You need to be arrested to prevent harm to yourself or someone else or
  • You may cause loss or damage to property or
 • You may commit an offence against public decency or cause an unlawful obstruction of the highway or
 • The police have reasonable grounds for believing that arrest is necessary to protect a child or other vulnerable person from you.
Despite the new powers the assumption is that the police should still proceed by way of summons for minor offences.

POWERS TO DETAIN

The police cannot keep a person at a police station to help them with their inquiries unless he has been arrested. They can, however, question anyone - but a person who attends a police station voluntarily cannot be forced to stay if he does not want to.

A person who is arrested must be told the grounds for the arrest. Once a person is charged police questioning must stop. Defendants are often detained for many hours without being charged while they and witnesses are questioned and evidence is studied.

No one can be detained for more than 24 hours without being charged unless an extension of 12 hours is authorised by a superintendent of police (which takes the time in custody up to 36 hours).

After that, an extension up to a maximum of 96 hours may be authorised by a magistrates court sitting in closed session after which the person in custody must be either charged or released.

While a person is in custody an application can be made for a writ of habeas corpus ("produce the body before the court") to secure his release if no charge is brought against him within a reasonable time.

If charged a defendant must either be granted police bail or be brought before a magistrates court no later than the next day (unless that day is a Sunday, Christmas Day or Good Friday).

The legislation permits terrorist suspects to be detained for longer than other suspects and for them to have fewer or more constrained rights.

The maximum period of detention without charge for someone arrested under terrorism legislation is 28 days but this is subject to judicial authorisation.

The criminal courts

Whether you have been summonsed for riding bike without lights or arrested on suspicion of murder, the legal process by which you are brought to justice starts at the magistrates court. This local court is the bottom rung of the criminal justice ladder which, in exceptional circumstances, could end at the Supreme Court, the highest court in the land. Here, starting from the bottom, are the courts that deal with criminal cases.

1. The Magistrates Court. Ninety-five per cent of criminal cases are started and finished in the magistrates court. Magistrates also deal with civil cases like family matters, liquor licensing and betting and gaming. Magistrates are appointed by the Crown and retire at 70 and there are about 30,000 in England and Wales. There are also about 130 District Judges – professionals once known as stipendiary magistrates - who sit alone and deal with the more complex or sensitive cases. Magistrates cannot normally send people to prison for more than 6 months (or 12 months for consecutive sentences), or fine people more than £5,000, so more serious cases are sent to the Crown Court.

2. The Youth Court: A specialised form of magistrates court that deals with people who were under 18 at the time it is alleged they committed the offence. Most young people have their cases dealt with in the youth court. The normal magistrates courts may deal with cases which involve people under 18 but only if they are tried with an adult. Young people also appear in the crown court if they are being jointly tried with an adult whose case needs to be heard in that court.

3. **The Crown Court** deals with more serious criminal cases such as murder, rape or robbery. Trials are heard by a judge and a 12 person jury. There are 77 crown courts across England and Wales. Appeals against a decision of the magistrates' court in criminal cases are also heard by the crown court. The Old Bailey, more correctly known as the Central Criminal Court, is a crown court.

4. The High Court of Justice is based at the Royal Courts of Justice in London but High Court judges 'on circuit' also sit in the larger provincial cities. They are the people who preside over the most serious cases at the crown court. The High Court also hears appeals on points of criminal law from both the magistrates court and the crown court.

5. The Court of Appeal Criminal Division, hears appeals from the crown court. The criminal division is presided over by the Lord Chief Justice and has jurisdiction over appeals by the defendant against conviction or sentence given at a trial in the crown court and deals with references by the Attorney General on a point of law after an acquittal or against an unduly lenient sentence.

6. The Supreme Court: The final court of appeal in criminal cases from England, Wales and Northern Ireland.

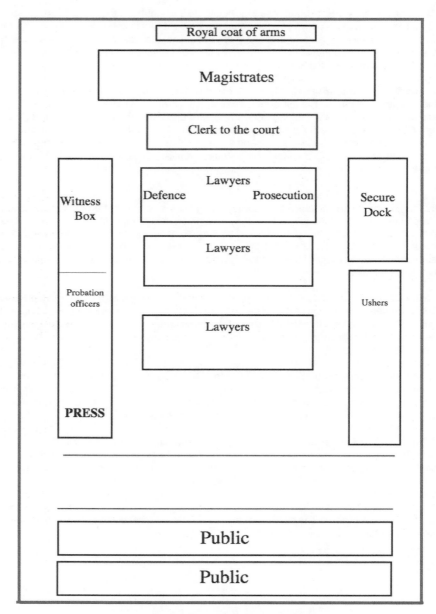

Floor plan of a typical magistrates court

Royal coat of arms: This signifies that criminal offences offend the community as a whole as represented by the Crown.

Magistrates: These are unpaid 'justices of the peace' appointed by the crown on the recommendation of local advisory committees. People are supposed to be judged by their peers but at one time magistrates were criticised as being 'middle-aged, middle-class, and white.' Now efforts are made to recruit magistrates who represent all sections of the community. Each case is decided by a 'bench' of at least two lay magistrates, usually three, one of whom is the chairman. Occasionally cases are heard and decided by a single person - a district judge (once known as a stipendiary magistrate) who is a professional lawyer.

Clerk to the court: The technical name for this post is legal advisor but most people still cling to the old name. This official records what goes on during the proceedings and also advises the magistrates on points of law.

Lawyers: Lawyers are either solicitors or barristers. Solicitors are all-rounders in law and the people that anyone in trouble goes to first. The solicitor may handle the case themselves or 'brief' a barrister who specialises in a particular branch of law. Most run-of--the mill cases are handled by solicitors. The prosecuting solicitor (or sometimes barrister) in a magistrates court is a member of the Crown Prosecution Service. The CPS, rather than the police, decides in most cases what the charges against the defendant will be and then provide the prosecuting lawyer.

Probation officers: When instructed by the court they interview offenders and prepare background reports so that magistrates have a clear picture before sentencing. They also supervise and guide people who have been given the chance of a specific period of probation, a duty which often brings media criticism when things go wrong.

Ushers: Black-robed, they are the people who usher witnesses and defendants in and out of the court room.

Public: Magistrates courts are open to the public.

Witness box: Where witnesses give evidence and where defendants who plead guilty to minor offences stand.

The media: Reporters only, no pictures allowed.

Secure dock: This is connected directly to the holding cells where people recently arrested or brought to the court while on remand in custody are kept while waiting to appear before the magistrates. The dock is usually constructed to be reasonably escape-proof while at the same time allowing prisoners to see and hear the proceedings clearly.

The people in the dock

The custody sheet below is dated January 1999 but could be, will be, replicated today and tomorrow. The people who occupy the secure dock at a typical magistrates court are a reflection of the social background to court reporting that reporters should be aware of.

SERIAL	NAME	FROM	SOLICITOR	TIME IN	INJURY	Signature
1.	ATKINSON (F)	POLICE	SCOTT	9 05	SPR WRIST	L. Atkinson
2. 5	WORSWICK	L F	EARNSHAW	0935		M. WESWICK
3.	SHARROCK	RISLEY	PRISONERS TO			
4. 6	KENNYON	P.P.	BE PRODUCED IN THE AFTERNOON DUE TO HMP			
5. 6	SULEMAN	P.P.				
6. 6	WHITESIDE	P P				
7. 8	ARMSTRONG	POLICE	LEACH	0920		ARMSTRONG
8. 8	SINGLETON (M)	POLICE	FORBES	0912		M Singleton
9. 7	ABRAMS	POLICE	DIDS	0720		
10. 7	McDERMOTT	POLICE	BRAILSFORD	0912		McDermott
11. 7	CLEMSON	POLICE	S. SCOTT	0720		
12. 8	BEAN	POLICE	J. ROBERTS (D'SOL)	0912		K. R.
13.	SWEENEY					
14.						
15.						
16.						
17.						
18.						
19.						
20.						

GROUP 4.   PRESTON MAGISTRATES COURT.

The first name Atkinson has a circled F next to it indicating that she is a woman. She also has a injury – a sprained wrist – recorded and signed for by her in case there are later any allegations of ill-treatment in the cells.

Sharrock, third down, is also a woman and is brought to the court from the then notorious Risley Remand Centre, known as Grisly Risley because of the number of suicides among people who had been remanded in custody and were waiting months for their trial in squalid, overcrowded conditions. Those remanded included people who were later found not guilty. The remand centre at Risley was closed down three months after this woman appeared and conditions for prisoners on remand have since improved as a result of the outcry over Grisly Risley.

Messrs Kennyon, Suleman and Whiteside could not appear in the court that morning and would have to arrive in the afternoon because they were lodged in Preston Prison where the warders were on strike. Besides confining prisoners to their cells, a warders' strike also disrupts the judicial system.

Prisoners 7,8,9,10,11,12 and 13 were all brought up from the cells in the police station next door to the court and had probably been arrested for offences the previous day and night. All of them had been seen by solicitors. No 8, Singleton, is 18 years old. Eighteen is the cut-off point between youth and adult offenders.

Sweeney, the last man, was seen by the duty solicitor, one of a number of local solicitors who form a rota to be called in by the police to give advice to people after their arrest.

The custody sheet was prepared by Group 4, one of the security firms who escort prisoners between the prisons and the courts and are also responsible for them during their time in court. Prior to this privatisation, escort and security duties were shared by the police and the prison warders.

Categories of cases

There are three categories of cases which come before magistrates and the categories basically determine whether the case will be heard in the magistrates court or be sent to the superior Crown Court.

Category 1
Less serious offences which are usually triable only at the magistrates court. These are the SUMMARY cases.

Category 2
Serious offences like theft or indecent assault which can be tried "EITHER WAY" - that is tried by the magistrates or by a judge and jury at the crown court. If it is an either-way offence the defendant has the right to choose at which court he is tried.

Category 3
The most serious offences like murder and rape which can only be tried on indictment at Crown Court. An INDICTABLE OFFENCE is one that may be tried by jury. The magistrates pass the case through to the crown court by a process known as committal.

When dealing with committal proceedings, it is the role of the Bench to decide whether a 'case to answer' (or 'prima facie case') exists on the basis of the prosecution statements.

In the vast majority of cases this will have been agreed beforehand by the defendant's representative, but where this is in dispute, the Bench must read, or have read to them, the entire prosecution case and then hear argument from the prosecution and defence before ruling on the issue. If the Court finds that there is no case to answer, the matter is discharged. If not, the case is committed to the Crown Court for trial.

Starting on the next page are extracts from a court sheet with the last names and street addresses of the accused deleted. The three entries illustrate the three types of cases that come before a magistrates court.

```
SIMON ████████
████████████████
MUCH HOOLE
PRESTON,
PR2 4QT
D006688/02 - 1
919503M/3062566 B13/10/72

SUMMONED ON 25/09/02
USED VEHICLE WITHOUT A TEST CERTIFICATE
PENALTY NOT EXCEEDING LEVEL 3, LEVEL 4
IF ADAPTED TO CARRY MORE THAN EIGHT
PASSENGERS
SEC 47 ROAD TRAFFIC ACT 1988
                              RK96 81300
DATE   PLEA  MODE OF TRIAL
23/10/02  NAP
```

SUMMARY: The defendant has been summoned by post to appear at the court. His offence, not having an MOT for his vehicle, is as low level a crime as you can get and must be dealt with by the magistrates. The man can't go to prison for this. The most the magistrates can do is fine him. If the vehicle can carry more than eight passengers they can fine him a little more. As you may guess he has not bothered with a solicitor.

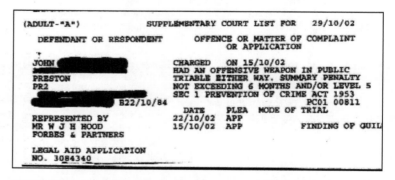

```
(ADULT-"A")            SUPPLEMENTARY COURT LIST FOR   29/10/02

DEFENDANT OR RESPONDENT     OFFENCE OR MATTER OF COMPLAINT
                                   OR APPLICATION

JOHN ████████████████    CHARGED   ON 15/10/02
                         HAD AN OFFENSIVE WEAPON IN PUBLIC
PRESTON                  TRIABLE EITHER WAY. SUMMARY PENALTY
PR2                      NOT EXCEEDING 6 MONTHS AND/OR LEVEL 5
                         SEC 1 PREVENTION OF CRIME ACT 1953
            B22/10/84                       PC01 00811
                         DATE    PLEA  MODE OF TRIAL
REPRESENTED BY           22/10/02  APP
MR W J H HOOD            15/10/02  APP             FINDING OF GUIL
FORBES & PARTNERS

LEGAL AID APPLICATION
NO. 3084340
```

EITHER-WAY: This is the third time John X has appeared at the magistrates court in connection with this particular case of having an offensive weapon in a public place. This is an "either-way" offence and when John X first appeared he had the choice of being tried by the magistrates or by a jury at the crown court. He opted for the magistrates court and was found guilty. The case was then presumably adjourned for reports. The maximum the magistrates can give him is six months. If they feel, in the light of the reports, which include any previous convictions, and the facts of the case, that six months is inadequate, they can send him to the crown court for sentencing. John is represented by the solicitor W.J. Hood and is on legal aid.

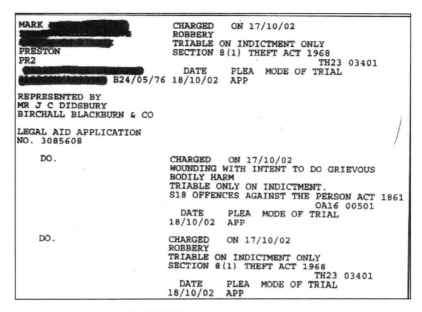

MARK ▓▓▓▓▓▓▓▓▓▓▓
▓▓▓▓▓▓▓▓▓▓▓▓
PRESTON
PR2
▓▓▓▓▓▓▓▓▓▓▓ B24/05/76

CHARGED   ON 17/10/02
ROBBERY
TRIABLE ON INDICTMENT ONLY
SECTION 8(1) THEFT ACT 1968
                        TH23 03401
DATE   PLEA MODE OF TRIAL
18/10/02 APP

REPRESENTED BY
MR J C DIDSBURY
BIRCHALL BLACKBURN & CO

LEGAL AID APPLICATION
NO. 3085608

DO.

CHARGED   ON 17/10/02
WOUNDING WITH INTENT TO DO GRIEVOUS
BODILY HARM
TRIABLE ONLY ON INDICTMENT.
S18 OFFENCES AGAINST THE PERSON ACT 1861
                        OA16 00501
DATE   PLEA MODE OF TRIAL
18/10/02 APP

DO.

CHARGED   ON 17/10/02
ROBBERY
TRIABLE ON INDICTMENT ONLY
SECTION 8(1) THEFT ACT 1968
                        TH23 03401
DATE   PLEA MODE OF TRIAL
18/10/02 APP

TRIABLE ONLY ON INDICTMENT: Mark X is facing two charges: 1. wounding with intent to do grievous bodily harm (GBH in courtroom parlance) and 2. robbery. These offences are too serious to be dealt with by the magistrates. They are 'triable only on indictment' and must go to the crown court. Mark X – represented by Mr JC Didsbury and on legal aid – has appeared once before, on the morning after the offences were allegedly committed. He would have been remanded then in custody until the court was able to start the legal process of sending him to the crown court.

Magistrates' powers

The magistrates can deal with cases in 12 ways. They are able to pick-and-mix as appropriate among the following powers. For instance, a vandal might be fined or sent to prison and also ordered to pay restitution for the damage he has caused.

1. Prison terms - but not for more than 6 months for any one offence nor for more than 12 months for more than one offence.

2. Suspended sentences - the offender does not have to go to prison unless he commits a further offence for which a prison sentence could be imposed during the time for which the first sentence is suspended.

3. Fines - maximum fines are fixed by statute for most offences.

4. Community service orders - an offender over the age of 16 is directed to work for a specified number of hours, without pay, for the good of the community.

5. Probation orders - an offender over the age of 17 is placed under the supervision of a probation officer for a specific period.

6. Absolute discharges - although the offender is guilty of an offence he is allowed to go free without any conditions attached.

7. Conditional discharges - again no penalty is imposed but if the offender commits another offence within a specified time he is liable to be dealt with for the first offence as well.

8. Bindings over - a defendant is bound over to be of good behaviour This typically happens with minor charges relating, say, to disputes between neighbours. If the defendant (or a witness or a complainant) agrees to be bound over the prosecution drops the case and no conviction is recorded.

9. Restitution orders - an offender makes good financially the damage he has caused.

10. Confiscation - of a vehicle used in furtherance of theft (which includes shoplifting).

11. Damages as compensation for personal injury or for loss or damage to goods.

12. They can send an offender to Crown Court for sentence after they have found a defendant guilty but feel that any sentence they can pass is inadequate.

Reporting the magistrates court

If you are reporting summary cases or either-way cases tried by the magistrates the report must include:

1. The name of the accused.
   His age.
   His address.

2. The offence of which he is accused, where it took place, when it took place

3. His plea - guilty or not guilty or, if is a preliminary session and no plea was entered, the fact that he was remanded - either in custody or on bail - to appear at the magistrates court at a future date.

4. The name of the magistrates court.

5. The decision of the magistrates - prison, fine, probation etc.

NB Always distinguish fines from costs ("He was fined £100 and ordered to pay £30 costs" not "He was fined £130").

Here is an example of a structure which fits most magistrates court cases. First-time reporters should try to keep each stage of the proceedings in its own compartment

A 27-year-old man who brandished a knife in the market square was fined £200 and ordered to pay £30 costs by Blanktown magistrates today.

Joe Bloggs, of 15, Somewhere Street, pleaded guilty to possessing an offensive weapon in a public place on March 23.

Mr Charlie Jones, prosecuting, said Bloggs drew the knife when a gang of youths shouted insults at his girlfriend.

Miss Kathleen Harris, representing Bloggs, said he had felt threatened by the gang and produced the knife to scare them away.

Mr Michael Hanratty, chairman of the magistrates, told Bloggs that knife crime was on the increase and must be punished.

All the essential details are contained in the first two sentences. The lawyers are reported in sequence and the chairman's remarks are the natural ending.

Reporting youth courts

Youth courts (previously known as juvenile courts) are a branch of the magistrates court that deal with young people who were under the age of 18 at the time they are alleged to have committed an offence. In law a 'child' is under 14 and a 'young person' is over 14 and under 18.

When a young person appears at a youth court - either as a defendant or a witness – he/she is automatically protected by **S49 Children and Young Persons Act 1933.**

S49 states that reports of a case at a youth court must not contain any particulars which could lead to the identification of any child or young person involved in the case as a defendant or witness. In particular it bans names and addresses, the name of the school the young person attends, and any photograph of the young person on the basis that, while young wrongdoers must be punished, it would be unfair to saddle them with bad publicity so early in their lives.

A hearing in the youth court is similar to one in the magistrates' court though the procedure is adapted to take account of age of the defendant and is less formal than in the magistrates..

Youth court sentences are designed to prevent further offending and include the making of a detention and training order of up to 2 years. A youth court may also send a young person to the crown court if the offence is very serious and the sentencing powers of the youth court are thought to be insufficient.

The court is not open to the general public and only those directly involved in the case will normally be in court. The press may attend and report the proceedings.

Lifting the identity ban:

The Crime Sentences Act 1997 gives a Youth Court the power to lift the ban on identifying a young person when he is convicted if the magistrates believe it would be in the public interest. The media can ask for the anonymity to be lifted.

Guidelines for the court include:

- the seriousness of the case or
- the persistent offending of the young person and
- whether warning the community about the offender's behaviour would help prevent further offences.

The magistrates must weigh those points against the possibility that printing the young person's name and address etc would put him or his family at risk and must also take into account the offender's age and vulnerability. They must also consider whether naming the offender would also reveal the identity of a vulnerable victim.

Lifting the identity ban as a form of extra punishment – 'naming and shaming' – is frowned upon.

Young people in adult courts

People under 18 can appear in the main magistrates court but only if they are tried alongside an adult. Young people also appear in the crown court if they are being jointly tried with an adult whose case needs to be heard in that court. Homicide and rape cases are always heard in the crown court.

Young people who appear in adult courts do not have their anonymity guaranteed. A ban on identifying the young prson has to be imposed by the magistrates or the judge via **S39 of the Children & Young Persons Act 1933.**

If a S39 order is issued it extends the identity ban not only to the defendant and witnesses but also to any other young person concerned in the proceedings – for instance a child who has been the victim of an assault.

The imposition of S39 orders is by no means automatic. Magistrates have to have good reasons for making them. Broadly this means balancing the public interest in knowing the identity of the young person against the harm public identification would do to him/her.

They give considerable weight to the age of the defendant while at the same time considering the public interest in knowing the identity of young people who have committed serious crimes. A boy aged 14 caught shoplifting trinkets with an adult is far more likely to have his identity protected than a 17-year-old youth who beat up an old age pensioner.

S39 orders apply only to the proceedings of the court that issues it. If a young person covered by a S39 order is sent from the magistrates to the crown court then the crown court must renew the order for its own proceedings.

Some magistrates courts issue S39 orders as a matter of course. Courts have also attempted to use S39 orders to ban the identity of young victims of abuse within families with the effect that the name of the adult defendant could not be published. The Court of Appeal, however, has stated that this action was wrong unless such defendants were themselves young persons under the age of 18.

Crown courts are often robust in refusing to renew S39 orders made by the magistrates, for example, when young people have been sent for trial or sentence charged with rape, murder, and robbery while on bail on a rape charge.

A S39 order only applies to people concerned in the proceedings and the effect of publicity on younger, blameless, relatives of the defendant is not grounds for granting one.

A S39 order lapses when the person reaches the age of 18.

The story on the next page is a good example of the issues involved in S39 orders.

Somerset County Gazette wins right
to name brawl-killing teenager

The Somerset County Gazette has won the right to name a teenager who delivered a fatal punch to a man in a street brawl earlier this year.

The Taunton-based Newsquest title persuaded Judge Graham Cottle, sitting at Exeter Crown Court, to lift an order under section 39 of the Children and Young Persons Act 1933 which had banned the media from naming Daniel Cain.

Cain, now 17, who was 16 at the time of the offence, and co-defendant Sean Wylds, 20, both of west Somerset, who were convicted of manslaughter in July, were given three-year custodial sentences on August 13.

The pair had launched an unprovoked attack on 36-year-old gardener Tim Chilcott in January, He was punched by Wylds then by Cain, suffering fatal head injuries when he fell to the ground.

At the time of the trial, the County Gazette faxed a letter to the court, setting out the paper's arguments for an application to lift the order.

The letter, drawn up by news editor Alex Cameron, argued that Cain should be identified because of the public interest in knowing who has committed serious offences, as a deterrent to others, and in the interests of open justice.

When the jury convicted the pair, Richard Smith, defending Cain, asked the court to delay consideration of whether to lift the order.

When the issue was raised on August 13 he argued that Cain should remain anonymous because of concerns for the rest of the teenager's family - his mother, stepfather and two young siblings, aged six and 10.

"What has come to light is a real concern for the rest of the family. They will consider removing themselves from the area and the village if the name is revealed because they feel it will be detrimental to the young children," he said.

Cameron told the judge that he felt it odd that the court was being asked to consider the family's welfare, when Cain clearly had not done so when he committed the offence, and also quoted the case in which Mr Justice Elias had said that the effect that naming a convicted juvenile would have on on family members should not normally be a relevant factor to be considered by a court.

Jigsaw identification

A child or a young person who is the victim in a sexual offence within the home and who is protected by a S39 order could still be identified if pieces of the identity jigsaw were provided by reports of the court case in different newspapers or broadcasts.

The local paper might give the name of the adult defendant and suppress details of the relationship with the victim while the local radio station could withhold the name of the defendant and give the full story of the offence.

Adding the two reports together would reveal the relationship and thus the identity of the young person.

The Press Complains Commission code of practice to avoid this situation is as follows:

In any press report of a case involving a sexual offence against a child:

- The adult should be IDENTIFIED.

- The term incest, where applicable, should not be used. The offence should be described as 'serious offences against children ' or similar appropriate wording.

- The child should NOT BE IDENTIFIED.

- Care should be taken that nothing in the report implies the relationship between the accused and the child.

This is a voluntary code. Any question of whether to depart from the code should always be referred to the editor.

Michael Stone retrial will be fair, rule judges

BY JOHN STEELE
CRIME CORRESPONDENT

MICHAEL Stone can receive a fair retrial in the hammer murders case because a new jury would have forgotten publicity about him after his original trial, or will be able to set aside anything they do recall, the Court of Appeal ruled yesterday.

Stone, 40, of Gillingham

the retrial "will not start until nearly three years after the publicity, which is the principal target of complaint, and people do forget.

. "Even if they do not forget entirely, the passage of time makes it easier for them to set aside that which they are told to regret."

He added that given that the central issue would be whether Daley could be

At first glance the various restrictions imposed on court reporting can be an intimidating tangle for the media law student. They begin to untangle once you realise the reasons they are there. The main object of all the rules and restrictions is simple. It is that an accused person gets a fair trial.

A fair trial is one where the guilt or innocence of the accused is judged solely on the evidence produced at the trial. There must also be a presumption that the accused has previously led an unblemished life. Totally innocent until proven guilty.

There cannot be a fair trial if the jury is seriously prejudiced against the accused because of something they have read in newspapers or heard on radio or television either before or during the trial.

There are two channels through which a jury might get information which results in them being prejudiced – for or against – the accused. One is through the media publishing sensational stories and backgrounders.

The other is through reports in the media of the various legal stages an accused must go through before he gets to plead not guilty at the crown court. There are three Parliamentary Acts which have a direct bearing on forthcoming jury trials.

The Contempt of Court Act 1981 covers media intrusion. This is dealt with separately in the book.

The Magistrates Court Act 1980 restricts what can be reported of pre-trial appearances.

The Bail Act 1976 sets out the rules by which magistrates decide whether the accused should get bail while he waits for the trial to start.

Reporting committals

As we have seen there are criminal offences - murder, rape, armed robbery etc – that are so serious that the magistrates do not have to power to deal with them. They must go to the crown court to be dealt with by judges and, when necessary, juries. In these cases the accused are automatically 'sent for trial' without the magistrates considering the evidence.

The process by which a person accused of an 'either way' offence is sent for trial is known as committal proceedings. Here the magistrates have to decide whether a 'case to answer' (aka 'prima facie' case) exists on the basis of the prosecution statements which have previously also been shown to the defence.

In the vast majority of cases these 'paper committals' go through without a hitch having been agreed beforehand by the defendant's solicitor. But where the defence considers that there is insufficient evidence to put the accused on trial the magistrates must read, or have read to them, the entire prosecution case and then hear argument from the prosecution and defence before ruling on the issue.

If the magistrates find that there is a case to answer, the accused is committed to the Crown Court for trial. If they find there is no case to answer the matter is discharged.

The Act restricting what can be reported of the committal process on the way to the trial at the crown court is the Magistrates Court Act 1980.

The provisions of this Act are designed to allow the case to be reported (justice must not only be done, it must be seen by the public to be done) but reported in such a way as to avoid prejudicing the future, all-important jury trial.

So **S8 of the Magistrates Courts Act 1980** limits the report of the committal to 10 factual points:

1. The name of the court and the names of the magistrates.

2. Names, addresses and occupations of parties and witnesses and the age of accused(s) and witnesses.

3. The offences with which the accused is charged, or a summary of them.

4. The names of barristers and solicitors in the case.

5. The decision of the court to commit the accused, or any of the accused for trial and any decisions on the disposal of the case of any accused not committed.

6. The charges on which the accused was committed, or a summary of them, and the court to which he was committed.

7. Where proceedings are adjourned the date and place to which they are adjourned.

8. Any arrangement as to bail.

9. Whether legal aid was granted.

10. Any decision of the examining magistrates to lift or not to lift the above reporting restrictions (1-9).

These restrictions can be lifted if:

1. The accused applies to have them lifted. If so they must be lifted.

2. The magistrates decide to commit none of the accused for trial.

3. The magistrates decide to try one or more of the accused summarily. If some accused are tried summarily and some are committed in the same proceedings the evidence relevant to those who have been tried summarily may be reported even if it impinges on the case of those sent for trial. If an accused is committed for sentence there are no restrictions on the report because he has already been tried summarily.

4. All the accused eventually have been tried at crown court. This means that evidence given at the committal, weeks earlier, can now be reported without waiting for any appeal. This delayed report of the committal proceedings, provided it is fair and accurate, will be treated as a contemporaneous report and will be protected.

5. It may be that in a case where there are two defendants one may want reporting restrictions lifted and his co-accused may not. If so, the examining magistrate may lift the restrictions only if he is satisfied that in the interests of justice it is right to do so.(Criminal Justice (Amendment) Act 1981).

Adding to the 10 points

Sometimes the media go beyond the 10 pieces of information allowed when reporting restrictions are imposed. For example:

1. When the accused chooses jury trial for reasons unconnected with the seriousness of the charge or his previous record. It may be a matter of principle. He may, for instance, have committed the offence in furtherance of a campaign and wants to be judged by a jury rather than magistrates. Newspapers have reported this type of situation to be fair to the accused.

2. The same is true when people complain of police treatment during questioning.

3. Newspapers and broadcasters anyway are constantly adding background to a court story even though reporting restrictions have not been lifted. They argue that such background is not itself a report of court proceedings and is not a contravention of the Act. (In that event the general rules of Contempt of Court still apply and will be discussed later).

In any event, the report **should in no circumstances mention previous convictions** or any other information that carries a serious risk of prejudicing the subsequent jury trial.

The question of bail

There is also the question of whether the accused should get bail while he waits for the trial to start: The rules governing bail applications are in the Bail Act 1976.

In theory this Act is biased in favour of the accused. At the time he is sent for trial the presumption must be that he is innocent of the offence with which he is accused.

It will take months for the trial to come to the crown court and if he is remanded in custody an innocent man could be cooped up behind bars all that time. (If he is found guilty the time spent in custody on remand reduces the eventual sentence.)

So under the Bail Act 1976 magistrates are required to remand the accused on bail unless they are satisfied that there are substantial grounds for believing he will :

* Abscond, commit other offences or interfere with the course of justice.

* He should be kept in custody for his own safety or he is already serving a prison sentence.

* There is not sufficient information available to make a decision.

Magistrates cannot grant bail to a person accused of homicide or rape if he has previously been convicted of such an offence.

The magistrates must give their reasons for refusing bail or, on the other hand, state their reasons for granting bail in the case of murder, manslaughter or rape. If bail is refused by magistrates the accused may apply to a judge in chambers.

The reporting of applications for bail also comes under S8 of the Magistrates Court Act. This restricts what may be reported to "arrangements as to bail on committal or adjournment".

This means the amount of any surety, any requirements to report to the police, the surrender of passport or any warning not to interfere with witnesses etc.

But the actual arguments as to whether bail should be granted cannot be published. Nor can the reasons for refusing bail which magistrates must give under the Bail Act 1976.

Therefore, the working rules for journalists are:

1. The report should in no circumstances mention previous convictions or any other information that carries a serious risk of prejudicing the subsequent jury trial.

2. The arguments for and against bail being granted must not be published.

3. The reasons for refusing bail, which (Bail Act 1976) the magistrates must give in court are also ruled out.

The crown court trial

THE LAWYERS

High Court Judges – There are 106 High Court judges and they try the more serious criminal cases in the provincial crown courts.

Circuit Judges: Some of the country's 600 circuit judges deal specifically with criminal cases at crown courts. They may also be asked to sit in the Criminal Division of the Court of Appeal.

Recorders are part-time judges whose jurisdiction is broadly similar to that of a circuit judge but they generally handle the less complex or serious matters.

Barristers and solicitors: Lawyers are either solicitors or barristers. It is barristers who prosecute at Crown Court trials and they usually appear for the defence but experienced solicitors who have gained higher court qualifications may also appear, titled solicitor advocates.

THE JURY

A jury is made up of 12 people aged between 18 and 70 chosen at random from the electoral list. Majority verdicts of 11-1 or 10-2 are allowed but only if the jury has failed to reach a verdict after at least two hours 10 minutes. If the numbers of a jury are reduced, say through illness, a majority of 10-1 or 9-1 is possible.

WITNESSES AND ANONYMITY

Unless it is necessary for evidential purposes witnesses need not disclose their addresses in open court but their names are usually given. There are times when the identity of witnesses are protected completely:

S11 of the Contempt of Court Act 1981 : This allows the court to ban the publication of any name or any other matter which has already been withheld from being mentioned in public during the court proceedings - for example the name of a blackmail victim or an undercover policeman.

Youth Justice and Criminal Evidence Act 1999 : S46 of the Act gives courts the power to ban the identification of a witness over the age of 18 during his lifetime. A court may make an order if it is satisfied that the quality of the witnesses evidence or the level of his co-operation would be diminished by fear or distress and that his evidence or cooperation would be improved if his identity were protected.

Evidence in Private: The Act also allows a court to take special measures to ease the strain on vulnerable or intimidated witnesses. These include excluding the public and all but one member of the Press while evidence is being given in a sexual offence case or where a person other than the accused might intimidate a witness.

THE ACCUSED

The charges are read out to the accused and he pleads either Guilty or Not Guilty.
Guilty: If the plea is Guilty, the prosecuting barrister outlines the evidence, reveals any past convictions of the accused, and presents any social inquiry reports about the

accused. The accused himself, or his lawyer, is then allowed to address the court before sentence is passed.

It may be that this speech of mitigation includes statements that are damaging to another person's character. If there are substantial grounds to believe that the statement is false, or irrelevant to the sentence, the court may order that the statement made in mitigation should not be reported for 12 months.

Not Guilty: If the accused pleads Not Guilty a jury is sworn in and the substance of the charges is read to them. The counsel for the prosecution then opens the case against the accused and outlines the evidence which will form the prosecution case.

The prosecution then calls its witnesses who give their evidence at the prompting of the prosecution lawyer and are then cross-examined by the defence lawyer.

The defence then begins to present its version of events and produces witnesses for the defence who are in turn cross-examined by the prosecuting counsel.

After all the evidence has been given, the prosecuting counsel makes his final speech to the jury and the defence lawyer addresses them last.

The judge then sums up the case for the jury and directs them as to the law involved but leaves the facts of the case to the jury unless he feels there is not enough evidence to support the charge and directs the jury to bring in a verdict of Not Guilty.

THE REPORTER

Great care should be taken about the way in which the opening address by the prosecution is reported. What the prosecuting counsel is saying is not in itself evidence. It is only a summary of what will be stated later by the prosecution witnesses. The preliminary claims therefore are precisely that, claims, and should not be reported as facts.

A prosecuting counsel may "allege" or "claim" that a policeman saw a gun and the report should read: The prosecuting counsel alleged that a policeman saw the accused with a gun.

When the policeman himself gives evidence the reporter can write: The policeman said: "I saw a gun."

After that the case can be reported in the usual way with the proviso that it should be fair and accurate if it is to be protected as far as Libel and Contempt of Court is concerned.

The requirements of 'fair and accurate' court reports are dealt with later in this section.

Anonymity: sex offences

The victims of sexual offences are more likely to report them to the police if they know their names will not be splashed across the media afterwards. The Sexual Offences (Amendments) Act of 1992 and 1976 combine to protect the identities of complainants alleging the following crimes:

Rape
Attempted rape
Aiding and abetting rape or attempted rape
Incitement to rape
Conspiracy to rape
Burglary with intent to rape

The restrictions come in two stages:
1. Once an allegation has been made no personal details or picture can be published in his or her lifetime if it is likely to identify the complainant as a victim.

2. After a person has been accused of a rape offence nothing likely to lead to the victim being identified as a complainant must be published during the victim's lifetime – unless the "victim" is later charged with perjury in relation to the original complaint.

The anonymity for the victim remains in force even if the allegation is later withdrawn or the accused is later tried for a lesser offence than rape. It also applies to victims of male rape.

A judge at a crown court may remove the anonymity if satisfied that it imposes an unreasonable restriction on the reporting of the trial and that it is in the public interest to do so. The judge may also lift the anonymity, on the application of the defence, to bring witnesses forward where he is satisfied the defence would otherwise be substantially prejudiced or the accused would suffer substantial injustice.

Since the passing of the Criminal Justice Act 1988 there has been no anonymity for rape defendants but publication of the identity of the defendant, combined with other details, could lead to the identification of the defendant, as where a husband is accused of raping his wife.

OTHER SEXUAL OFFENCES

The 1992 Act provides a similar two-stage anonymity for complaints in such offences as:

Sexual Intercourse with a mentally-handicapped person.
Sexual intercourse with a child under 13.
Incest, indecent assault etc.

The restrictions can be lifted by a magistrate or a judge is he feels they unreasonably restrict reporting the case. The anonymity can be lifted with the complainant's written consent.

CIVIL CASES

The anonymity for life does not automatically apply to reports of civil proceedings - for example, a claim for damages for rape or to allegations made to an industrial tribunal.

Contempt issues

S4(1) Contempt of Court Act 1981
as it applies to court reporting

Imagine for a moment that you live in a small town which also contains a man who is constantly in trouble with the police. The numerous court cases in which he has been involved have all been recorded your newspaper. All your readers know that this man has convictions for minor violence. Now he has been charged with robbery with violence and must go to the crown court for trial.

You limit your report of the committal to the 10 factual points allowed by S8 of the Magistrates Courts Act 1980. But still , because of all the court reports in your paper about him, people who may be on the jury when he comes for trial cannot help but know that he's got previous convictions, that most lingering of all prejudicial information.

So is your newspaper responsible for contempt of court for , over a period of time, informing a potential juror that our violent friend has form? The answer, of course, is No.

S4(1) of the Contempt of Court Act 1981 gives immunity from contempt proceedings provided the court reports the newspaper or the radio programme previously published were:

Fair and accurate and published contemporaneously
(which means the first available edition or programme).

A real-life example of S4(1) is that of the serial killers Fred and Rosemary West, above, who together sexually assaulted and then murdered 10 young women. Fred West hanged himself while on remand in prison . Rosemary West pleaded not guilty to the 10 murders but was found guilty at Winchester Crown Court and sentenced to life imprisonment.

Earlier, when both were brought before Gloucester magistrates court and committed for trial at the crown court all that could be reported were the 10 points in S8 of the Magistrates Court Act 1980. As we have noted, one of the gravest prejudices that can be planted in the mind of a juror is the fact that the accused has a previous conviction for the same offence or some similar offence. Years before, the local Gloucestershire Echo had reported a court case in which the couple were convicted for sexually assaulting a 17-year-old girl.

The Gloucestershire Echo was perfectly entitled to report the sexual assault case when it happened (contemporaneously) but - and this is the crux of it - if they had dug out the cutting of the court report and used it again before the murder trial they would have been publishing material that would prejudice the mind of a juror.

They would have no defence to a contempt of court charge because the report did not comply with the requirements of S4(1). So the Gloucestershire Echo and other journalists in the know had to sit on that intriguing piece of information until Rose West's murder trial was over.

S4(2) Contempt of Court Act 1981 and the hierarchy of courts

The Rosemary West case was an example of the potential for 'long ago' court reports to prejudice a trial. But there is also the danger of contemporary legal proceedings having the same effect.

There is a hierarchy of courts under the umbrella of the '81 Act. All the criminal courts, all the civil courts, inquests, a variety of tribunals, mental health review panels - they are all classed as courts. Top of the pile are the criminal courts where people's liberty is at stake.

So what happens, then, if an inquest into the death of people involved in a a road accident is held just weeks before the trial at the crown court of one of the drivers who is accused of causing death by dangerous driving? The evidence given at the inquest could easily be read by a potential juror and might have a prejudicial effect.

In those circumstances the coroner could impose a S4(2) order postponing publication of reports of the evidence given at the inquest in order to avoid a substantial risk of serious prejudice at the crown court trial.

Before imposing a S4(2) order, the coroner would have to balance the risk of prejudice against the public's right to open justice. Broadly, the coroner would have to assess how substantial would be the risk of serious prejudice.

If a S4(2) order was imposed, the media would still be able to publish the inquest verdict and evidence after the crown court case had been completed.

Libel issues

A fair and accurate report, published contemporaneously of UK court proceedings held in public attracts **Absolute** privilege and is immune from an action for libel. **Qualified** privilege protects fair and accurate reports of court proceedings which are not published contemporaneously.

FAIR AND ACCURATE

If the report is unfair or inaccurate it forfeits both Absolute or Qualified privilege.
Example: In 1993 The Sunday Sport paid substantial out of court damages in a libel action brought by to a police officer based on the paper's reporting of a court case in which he had been found not guilty of indecent assault. The paper had reported the opening statement by the prosecution and the main evidence of the alleged victim but did not include her cross-examination by the defence which began the same day. During the cross-examination the alleged victim made a number of admissions which weakened the evidence she had given earlier and which the paper had reported. The Sunday Sport then briefly reported the policeman's acquittal but they neglected to report the admissions which effectively negated much of the adverse publicity the policeman had received in the earlier report.

CONTEMPORANEOUS

If the court report is not published contemporaneously - roughly the next reasonably available edition of the paper or the next television or radio news bulletin - it loses Absolute privilege but is still protected by Qualified privilege if all the conditions attaching to that defence are met.

These are that the report is:

Fair and accurate
Published without malice
On a matter of public concern
And the publication is for the public benefit

When might this protection be needed as far as court reporting is concerned? Say the chairman of the council's road safety committee is arrested for drink driving and his case is heard when there is no reporter at the magistrates court to report his conviction.
Some weeks later you hear that he has been banned from driving. You get the details of the case but you have already lost Absolute privilege because the report will not be contemporaneous with when the case was heard.

What you still have left is qualified privilege with its four requirements listed above but particularly that his conviction was a matter of public interest and that publishing the report was for the public benefit.

Remember that privilege is restricted to reports of the court proceedings only. Documents seen by the judge or magistrates but not read in open court are not covered but there is qualified privilege for fair and accurate copies of, or extracts from, documents made available by the court.

The civil courts step by step

The Royal Courts of Justice in The Strand, London

Civil courts resolve disputes between individuals or companies, mostly over money, but areas such as the welfare of children, matrimonial disputes, the settlement of wills and libel actions also feature in the case-load.

1. Magistrates Court: This has a rather limited function in civil matters, mostly confined to family proceedings. Magistrates have the power to make a number of orders for the welfare of a child. They also issue anti-social behaviour orders and hear licensing appeals.

2. County Court: Often referred to as the Small Claims Court, it deals mostly with cases between people or companies who believe that someone owes them money. Claims for things like breach of contract , damage to property, traffic accidents, personal injury and faulty goods are common as are disputes over housing , including mortgage and council rent arrears and re-possession.

The judgments which relate to payment of money are recorded on the Register of County Court Judgments and the information is used by banks, building societies and credit companies to check an individual's credit-worthiness.

The county court – there are 216 of them throughout England and Wales - also deals with Family issues such as divorce or adoption. Family proceedings are mostly dealt with by district judges but circuit judges deal with the more serious cases.

3. The High Court deals with the more important civil disputes in which large sums of money or other important issue are at stake. It is based at the Royal Courts of Justice, but may also sit at 'first tier' Crown Court centres across England and Wales. There are three divisions of the High Court:

The Queen's Bench Division deals, broadly, with actions for damages arising

of contract such as failure to complete work on time or pay money due for work done and, importantly for the media, libel.

The Family Division deals with Children Act proceedings, wardship and adoption applications, divorce and ancillary relief proceedings and declarations in medical treatment cases. It also deals with wills and, where no will has been made, the distribution of estates under the intestacy laws (See: Family proceedings later).

The Chancery Division covers property. intellectual property, patents, trade marks, copyright, insolvency, commercial frauds and business disputes. The Division is increasingly involved with financial regulatory work and professional negligence.

4. The Appeal Court Civil Division hears appeals from the High Court and (directly by-passing the High Court) from the county courts. There are 37 regular judges of the Court of Appeal whose title is either Lord Justice or Lady Justice. The Master of the Rolls is the President of the Court of Appeal, Civil Division. He is also Head of Civil Justice.

5. The Supreme Court: The Court of Appeal may refer cases involving points of law to the Supreme Court where the Justices, if they follow their practice in the House of Lords, will usually sit in panels of five.

Categories of civil cases

Most civil cases centre on money and they all begin with a claim form. The form sets out the details of the claimant's case and the amount they are seeking and is served on the defendant.

There are two choices open to the defendant:

1. He can decide not to file any defence to the claim and judgment against him is entered by the court 'in default'. As soon as the judgment is entered the claimant may use the court's services to enforce it.

2. If the defendant decides to fight the case he must file his defence within 28 days. The case is then allocated to one of three tracks:

Small claims – below £5,000. These cases should be decided by a district judge within three months.

Fast track - £5,000 - £15,000. These cases should be heard within 30 weeks and the court proceedings should last no more than a day.
An example is the procedure for libel. Major libel cases are usually heard by a judge and jury but if plaintiffs are willing to accept damages of £10,000 or less they can take advantage of the 'fast track' procedure. In a suitable case a plaintiff wanting a quick apology and modest damages will not be forced to incur huge legal costs in getting them. Claims are dealt with by a judge without a jury and – if successful – the claimant can get any or all of the following remedies:.

- Declaration that the statement was false and defamatory
- Order to publish suitable correction and apology
- Damages not exceeding £10,000
- Injunction restraining further publication

Multi-track – the more complex cases. Efforts are made to resolve the dispute by negotiation or mediation but if this fails a trial is arranged.

These are the people who deal with civil cases in the first instance.....
High Court judges try important civil cases which are divided among the three divisions of the High Court according to their nature.

Circuit judges: Some circuit judges deal specifically with civil cases, while some are authorised to hear public and/or private family cases. Others may sit more or less on a full-time basis in specialised civil jurisdictions, such as chancery or mercantile cases, or as judges of the Technology or Construction Court.

Recorders: Recorders' jurisdiction is broadly similar to that of a circuit judge, but they generally handle less complex or serious matters coming before the court.

District Judges: Each county court has one or more district judges who deal in open court with fast track and small claims and privately with land and family disputes.

Family proceedings

Family Proceedings are a minefield of emotion and controversy especially when adults are arguing over the future of children.

These proceedings are heard in all three civil courts, magistrates, the county court and the Family Division of the High Court. The Children's Act 1989 empowers these courts to make orders to ensure the welfare of children under 18.

There are various orders which determine disputes over who should care for the child in the future, what access to the child should other people be allowed, how and where the child should be educated and many other contentious issues including affiliation orders for the maintenance of the child.

Applications for these orders are mainly made by two sets of people:,

1. By social services who have been alerted to concerns over the child's welfare.

2. By parents who are divorcing or separating.

Fundamental to the reporting of these cases is the right to privacy of the child involved.

MEDIA ACCESS TO FAMILY PROCEEDINGS

Before April 2009, the media was allowed into family cases only in the magistrates courts (except for adoption cases) and the Court of Appeal. Hearings in the County Court and the High Court were held in private.

This secrecy led to campaigns for more openness. In matrimonial cases some losing parents felt aggrieved at decisions over contact with their children and accused the courts of bias behind closed doors. Where social workers were concerned there was a belief that some of them were too quick to jump to conclusions about parents and were able to get away with mistakes because of the lack of open scrutiny in the courts.

The changes introduced in April 2009 were as follows:
• Accredited media (holders of a UK press card) may be admitted to family courts (county courts and the High Court) that were formally closed removing the discrepancy with the already open magistrates' courts and the Court of Appeal.

• No bloggers, occassional newsletter writers or foreign media not based in the UK will be given such access.

* All existing court-reporting restrictions apply, protecting the anonymity of children and preventing mention of names, places and possibly also local authorities where that would identify children.

• The media have no automatic right to evidence or documents relied on in court.

• There is still no admittance to adoption proceedings or hearings held for "judicially-assisted conciliation and negotiations".

BASIC RULES

Even when the press is allowed to remain it is an offence under S97 of the Children's Act 1989 to publish anything likely to identify a child involved in the proceedings.

All that can be published are:

1. The names and addresses and occupations of the adults involved.

2. The grounds of the application and a concise statement of the charges, defences and counter charges.

3. Any submission on a point of law and the court's decision on it.

4. The decision of the court and any observations by the court in making it.

WARDS OF COURT

Wardship applications are heard in the county court and the High Court and the ward of court has anonymity under the Children's Act but the media can write stories about a particular case providing the child is not identified as a ward of court.

Asbos: a case history

The social implications of changes in the law continue long after the law is passed and put into operation. This is how the local press reacted on November 1, 2006 after Warwickshire Police decided on a policy of publishing the photographs and details of people against whom Anti-social Behaviour Orders, Asbos, had been made.

One of those pictured was aged 14, one aged 15, two aged 16 and three aged 17.

The very next day the Guardian published an article with the headline:'Teenagers see Asbos as badge of honour'.

The intro read: "Anti-social behaviour orders are widely seen as "badges of honour" by offending teenagers, their parents and even some criminal justice professionals, and fail in nearly half of all cases, according to an officially commissioned study published today."

Asbos are an example of Parliament making laws to deal with on-going social problems. Throughout the 1990s the public was becoming stridently fed up with loutish and unruly conduct that was making life misery for people in local communities. The Labour government's reaction was to introduce Asbos as a key part of the Crime and Disorder Act 1998, a central plank of Labour's law and order policy.

Asbos are imposed for a term of between two and five years and most commonly include bans on causing harassment, alarm or distress, exclusion zones from particular places or parts of town, and bans on mixing with other named individuals.

Legally they are unusual because they are imposed in a civil court but trangressions of the Asbo are punished in a criminal court.

This is because dealing with louts in the criminal courts means producing first hand, eye-witness evidence which many of the sufferers were unwilling to provide on the basis that it might make matters worse. Parliament got round that by making the Asbo a civil, not a criminal, matter. This meant that people did not have to face their tormentors in court.

Instead, 'hearsay' evidence - unacceptable ina criminal court - could be collected from them by either the police or the local authority and presented to the magistrates court sitting in its civil capacity.

The sting in the tail was that breach of an Asbo also became a criminal offence. The maximum penalty is five years imprisonment for an adult or a two-year detention and training order for juveniles, 12 months of which is custodial.

The standard of proof required where a breach of the order is concerned is the criminal standard. Guilt must be established beyond reasonable doubt. Where groups of people are engaged in anti-social behaviour a case needs to be made against each individual against whom an order is sought but the cases can be heard together by the court.

Today miscreants are at risk of getting an Asbo if they do any of the following:

Graffiti.
Abusive and intimidating language, often directed at minorities.
Excessive noise, particularly late at night.
Fouling the street with litter.
Dealing drugs.
Harassment of residents or passers-by.
Verbal abuse.
Criminal damage.
Vandalism.
Threatening behaviour in large groups.
Racial abuse.
Smoking or drinking alcohol under age.
Substance misuse.
Joyriding.
Begging.

Prostitution.
Kerb-crawling.
Throwing missiles.
Assault.
Vehicle crime.

In September 2009 the Government added another to the list. - so-called Booze Asbos aimed at people in England and Wales who commit crimes or behave anti-socially while drunk. Police and councils can now seek a Drinking Banning Order on anyone aged 16 and over. Magistrates can then ban them from pubs, bars, off-licences and certain areas for up to two years. Anyone who breaches an order faces a £2,500 fine.

These are the courts that can make Asbos:

• Magistrates' courts (acting in their civil capacity)

• County courts (where the principal proceedings involve anti-social behaviour)

• Magistrates' courts (on conviction in criminal proceedings)

• The Crown Court (on conviction in criminal proceedings)

• Youth courts (on conviction in criminal proceedings)

The order 'bolted' on the back of a criminal conviction is known as a Crasbo, short for criminal anti-social behaviour order.

ORDERS AGAINST CHILDREN AND YOUNG PEOPLE

An order can be made against anyone aged 10 years or more who has acted in an anti-social manner and where an order is needed to protect people from any repetition. Applications for Asbos against juveniles can be heard in the magistrates' court.

They are not heard in the youth court as a matter of course because of the civil status of the orders, although youth courts may, as indicated above, make orders where appropriate on conviction.

Automatic reporting restrictions would apply under S49 of the Children and Young Persons Act 1933 to orders made on conviction in the youth court, but there are no automatic reporting restrictions in the magistrates' courts against juveniles.

A court making an Asbo does have the power under S39 of the Children and Young Persons Act 1933 to impose restrictions to protect the identity of a person under 18. But reporting restrictions may cancel out the effectiveness of the order which largely depends on the wider community knowing the details.

As the Guardian reported, there are serious reservations about the effectiveness of Asbos made against young people.

Research for the government's Youth Justice Board revealed that many involved in tackling youth offending, including magistrates, questioned how much they change the behaviour of teenage tearaways.

Enforcing the orders has often proven difficult, so to encourage the public to take an active role recipients are frequently "named and shamed" (as illustrated in the Warwickshire paper).

Between April 1999 and December 2004, a total of 4,649 Asbos were issued in England and Wales and that number rose by over 100pc by the end of 2005 to 9,853. By December 2007 14,972 Asbos had been issued.

In February 2007, the government, in response to a freedom of information request, revealed that 47pc of these orders have been breached. Later figures revealed that 55 per cent of the 17,000 Asbos issued between June 2000 and December 2008 were breached, leading to an immediate custoodial sentence in more than half the cases.

Those working in local youth offending teams and some magistrates regard the high level of non-compliance as a key indicator that the orders are not only ineffective, but that they also increase the long-term risk of the teenager being jailed.

In July 2010 Asbos became a political issue. Theresa May, Home Secretary in the new coalition government, launched a review of the system and said it was time to move beyond Asbos, time to "stop tolerating" bad behaviour.

Mrs May said she wanted a review of the powers because police should be able to use their common sense to deal with anti-social behaviour. Punishments should be rehabilitative and restorative, rather than criminalising, she argued.

"We need a complete change in emphasis, with people and communities working together to stop bad behaviour escalating.,We need to make anti-social behaviour what it once was, abnormal and something to stand up to, rather than frequent and tolerated."

For Labour, shadow home secretary Alan Johnson said: "An anti-social behaviour order is one of a series of different powers available to the police and is used when other punitive measures have failed.

"Of course it is right to keep such matters under review to ensure the public has speedy access to measures to stop anti-social behaviour. However, there is no doubt that the introduction of Asbos have made a huge contribution towards tackling crime and anti-social behaviour."

It will be up to ministers in Scotland and Northern Ireland to decide what, if anything, to do with Asbos as they are a devolved matter in those countries.

PRIVATE & CONFIDENTIAL

PRIVACY LAW STEP BY STEP

On the right, Naomi Campbell, super-model. On the left, Naomi Campbell, recovering drug-addict. Two pictures which illustrate the battle between the media and celebrities over privacy. Ms Campbell was perfectly happy for the Mirror to use the glamour shot. When they used the other picture she sued.

Campbell's court case against the Mirror - which will be discussed in detail later - was a major landmark in the rapidly developing code of privacy in the UK.

It started after the Mirror used the picture of Campbell outside a drugs rehabilitation centre. Campbell claimed that the picture amounted to a breach of confidence and was also a violation of her rights under the Human Rights Act and the Data Protection Act

The fact that she was able to sue under three different headings shows how dramatically the law relating to privacy has changed in the last decade or so.

It was not always so easy for a celebrity to sue. When Gordon Kaye crashed in his car during a storm on Burns' Night in January 1990 his head injuries were so severe that surgeons had to carry out emergency brain operations. While lying in his hospital bed recovering from the surgery - and still only semi-conscious -   the 'Allo, 'Allo star was "interviewed" and photographed by Sunday Sport journalists disguised as medical staff.

It was an outrageous invasion of his privacy but when Kaye sought to bring an action against the paper it became apparent that there was no law of privacy in the UK that covered his case.

At that time all that existed was the Law of Confidence which protected information passed between people in established relationships like lawyer and client, husband and wife, doctor and patient.

If Kaye's doctor, perish the thought, had passed information to the Sunday Sport Kaye would have been able to sue the doctor for breach of an established confidential relationship. Kaye had no such relationship with the Sunday Sport journalists so could not claim breach of confidence.

But then came the Human Rights Act 1998 and everything changed. A citizen's right to respect for private and family life was enshrined. Judges were quick to use the Human Rights Act to adjust the existing law of confidence so that breach of confidence was no longer dependent on there being an established relationship between the whistle-blower and the victim.

Just a month after the Act was introduced in October 2000, Lord Justice Sedley said *(Douglas v Hello! Ltd)* that its terms indicated that the law had to protect not only people whose trust had been abused but also people (like Gordon Kaye?) who had found themselves subjected to an unwanted intrusion into their personal lives.

Then (again perhaps with Kaye in mind) he said: "The law no longer needs to construct an artificial relationship of confidentiality between intruder and victim."

That was the big step one on the path towards a law of privacy – there was now no need for an established relationship. Gordon Kaye could have sued the Sunday Sport for breach of confidence.

Another giant step came in 2004 when the House of Lords made a distinction between information that was 'confidential' in the true sense of that word and information that was more correctly termed 'private', with both types warranting protection.

So developed two legal remedies for unauthorised use of information, both under the wide umbrella of the Law of Confidence. Drawing that distinction was more than semantics. It led to two different methods of approaching privacy cases.

Unlike Libel, there are no hard and fast rules by which privacy cases are decided. Areas of Libel such as Fair Comment and Statutory Privilege have precise rules which must be satisfied if the defences are to be gained.

That is not the case with privacy. Instead, each case is exposed to what the law calls "intense focus upon the individual facts."

This approach of applying an intense focus to each case is incompatible with broad generalisations such as "public figures must expect to have less privacy" or "people in positions of responsibility must be seen as role models".

This has had a big impact on media who feed off the culture of celebrity and were previously restrained only by the laws of libel. The framework within which the intense focus is directed is broadly as follows:

1. The law will protect information which is "obviously private" or where there is a "reasonable expectation" of privacy. The question central to each case is:

Was there a reasonable expectation that the information would remain private?

The court looks at:

> a. The nature of the information – whether it is merely titillation or more serious matter.

> b. The way in which it is displayed – the more lurid the coverage the more likely it will be restrained.

> c. The relationship between the discloser and the 'victim'.

Importantly, it considers the coverage by the distressing affect it would have on the victim and family alone rather than on the reaction of the man in the street. On the other side, publication of private information can be justified in the public interest.

The legal procedures involved in dealing with privacy issues will be dealt with in detail later but first it is useful to understand the implications for the media of the rapidly developing privacy law...........the clash between the media's idea of public interest and the law's widening interpretation of what is, and what is not, "private and confidential".

The clash between free expression for the media and privacy for the celebrity is graphically illustrated by The People's reaction to an injunction. Meanwhile, next page, Daily Mail editor Paul Dacre decides to get personal...........

'As cold as a frozen haddock, Mr Justice Eady hands down his views shorn of moral balance...'

" During the lurid case of Mosley v News of the World, there was only one moment when Mr Justice Eady betrayed his humanity.

It came when the editor of the red-top tabloid described how busy his office tends to be on Friday evenings.

'You have a lot of balls in the air,' he said.

It was not, perhaps, the most felicitous phrase in a hearing which detailed a 'sex party' involving motor-racing chief Max Mosley and several under-dressed women, some speaking 'Allo 'Allo-style German.

'Balls in the air' indeed. A wintry smile crept on to the lean lips of Mr Justice Eady.

But then it disappeared as fast as it had arrived. For the rest of the case, he remained as cold as a frozen haddock.

Sir David Eady doesn't 'do' emotion. He doesn't really 'do' anything except the strict letter of the law, even when that law is palpably asinine.

Reporters at the Royal Courts of Justice groaned when they heard he would be deciding the News of the World case. He has a reputation, rightly or wrongly, of being anti-Press."

It was not the kind of deferential press usually accorded to High Court judges but the gloves were off as far as the Daily Mail was concerned.

Columnist Quentin Letts was playing back-up to his editor, Paul Dacre, who chose the annual conference of the Society of Editors to accuse Sir David of personally bringing in a privacy law by the back door with a series of 'arrogant and amoral' judgements.

The judge had already incurred the wrath of national newspaper editors in 2004 when he gave Maxine Carr, the girlfriend of the Soham murderer Ian Huntley, the right to privacy for life and, two years later, when he prevented the media from exposing a football celebrity's affair with a married woman, saying that the lovers had the right to privacy.

And in any event, he said, the woman's husband was seeking to expose the affair out of revenge and because he would be paid by the newspaper..

The decision that lit the touch-paper of Dacre's wrath was the case of Max Mosley v News

Group Newspapers in which Eady concluded that the News of the World had no right to expose Formula One chief Max Mosley's S&M orgy with five prostitutes. Mr Mosley's behaviour, said the judge, was merely "unconventional". Mr Dacre wondered if Sir David would have felt the same way if one of the women had been his wife or daughter. The News of the World story had been headlined:

F1 BOSS HAS SICK NAZI ORGY WITH 5 HOOKERS
Son of Hitler-loving fascist in sex shame

"FORMULA One motor racing chief Max Mosley is today exposed as a secret sado-masochist sex pervert.

The son of infamous British wartime fascist leader Oswald Mosley is filmed romping with five hookers at a depraved NAZI-STYLE orgy in a torture dungeon.

Mosley – a friend to F1 big names like Bernie Ecclestone and Lewis Hamilton – barks ORDERS in GERMAN as he lashes girls wearing mock DEATH CAMP uniforms and enjoys being whipped until he BLEEDS."

In his judgement Eady said he had to consider whether Mosley's behaviour - described by the News of the World's lawyers as immoral, depraved and to an extent adulterous - could be a matter of legitimate journalistic investigation or public interest. He concluded that it could not:

"It is not for the state or for the media to expose sexual conduct which does not involve any significant breach of the criminal law," he said.

" It is not for journalists to undermine human rights, or for judges to refuse to enforce them, merely on grounds of taste or moral disapproval. Where the law is not breached the private conduct of adults is essentially no-one else's business. The fact that a particular relationship happens to be adulterous, or that someone's tastes are unconventional or 'perverted', does not give the media carte blanche."

Eady's contention that adulterous relationships were essentially no-one else's business infuriated Dacre. He described Eady's judgement as " an unashamed reversal of centuries of moral and social thinking. He has placed the rights of the adulterer above society's age-old belief that adultery should be condemned."

The legal establishment – and many up-market press commentators - rallied to the defence of Eady. Desmond Browne QC, the chairman of the Bar Council, said there was a compelling case that newspapers should not be able to ride roughshod over privacy rights.

HUMAN RIGHTS ACT PITCHES FREE EXPRESSION AGAINST PRIVACY

On the one hand there is the desirability of a free press, the watchdog of the public, being protected by the right to free expression under Article 10.

On the other hand, there is the desirability of people who want to keep some some private information to themselves being protected by the right to privacy under Article 8.

This tension between the two articles is most marked in the battle over privacy between media and celebrity. Many celebrities live by publicity. What they have to sell is themselves, their personal appearance and their personality. They employ public relations agents to present their personal life to the media in the best possible light. That is no criticism of them. It is a trade like any other. But it does mean that their relationship with the media is different from that of people who expose less of their private life to the public.

ARTICLE 10: FREEDOM OF EXPRESSION

(1) Everyone has the right of freedom of expression. This right shall include freedom to hold opinions and to receive and impart information and ideas without inference by public authority and regardless of frontiers. This Article shall not prevent States from requiring the licensing of broadcasting, television or cinema enterprises.

(2) The exercise of these freedoms, since it carries with it duties and responsibilities, may be subject to such formalities, conditions, restrictions or penalties as are prescribed by law and are necessary in a democratic society, in the interests of:

> * National security, territorial integrity or public safety,
> * for the prevention of disorder or crime,
> * for the protection of health or morals,
> * *for the protection of the reputation or rights of others,*
> * *for preventing the disclosure of information received in confidence,*
> * or for maintaining the authority and impartiality of the judiciary.

The lines in italics provide the limits to free expression in privacy cases as far as the media is concerned although there have been cases where national security (the *Spycatcher* case) and the prevention of disorder or crime (the *Bulger* case discussed later) have led to injunctions forbidding publication. This is how it works out with the lines in italics:

> 1. The long-established laws of libel look after the protection of *reputation*.
>
> 2. The *'rights of others'* are those contained in the European Convention - respect for family life, privacy in public places, the financial exploitation of private photographs, threat to life, threat of torture have all featured under the generic heading of 'privacy' cases.
>
> 3. The *disclosure of information* received in confidence is the basis of most privacy cases.

ARTICLE 8: RIGHT TO PRIVACY

1. Everyone has the right for his private and family life, his home and his correspondence.

2. There shall be no interference by a public authority with the exercise of this right except such as is in accordance with the law and is necessary in a democratic society in the interests of:

* national security, public safety or the economic well-being of the country,

* for the prevention of disorder or crime,

* for the protection of health or morals,

(The three above can be brought together under 'public interest')

* or for the protection of the rights and freedoms of others.

(The 'rights of others' include the media's right to free expression under art.10)

In simple terms, therefore, the conflict in privacy cases can be reduced to:

The media's freedom of expression can be trumped by a person's right to privacy which can itself be trumped by the public interest in the disclosure of the information.

The rules for injunctions

Once confidential information is published the damage has been done - so as soon as the 'victim' gets wind of impending publication his lawyers are likely to apply immediately for an injunction. An injunction is a court order forbidding publication of material either in the short term (an interim injunction) or permanently.

Claimants can apply for an injunction to prevent publication of the story in the first place or to prevent further publication if the story has already been published.

If the claimant succeeds in getting an interim injunction this sometimes kills the story for good without the claimant having to prove his case for confidentiality. Legal issues can take months to resolve and by that time the information may be stale or the story may have been overtaken by events and the media no longer bother to contest the injunction.

On the other hand, if the media can fight off the application for an interim injunction, the claimant may very well decide the issue was not worth taking to trial because the trial would only afford even more publicity to the story.

For these reasons the issuing of injunctions is a very important point of privacy law. So much so that when the Human Rights Act was being debated, the media lobbied MPs to ensure that injunctions could not be issued without media challenge.

The result was S12 of the Act which outlines the factors a duty judge must take into account when considering whether to grant an injunction – do not forget that injunctions are often applied for "out of office hours', sometimes over the phone, sometimes late at night before the first editions get off the press. These are the rules:

> 1. If the newspaper is not present or represented at the hearing then an injunction can not be granted unless the court is satisfied:
>
> *a. The person applying for the injunction has taken every practicable step to notify the newspaper about the hearing or*
>
> *b. There are compelling reasons why the newspaper should not be notified.*
>
> 2. No injunction should granted unless the court is satisfied that the applicant is finally likely to be able to establish that publication should not be allowed.
>
> 3. During it all the court must have regard to:
>
> *a. the importance of the media's right to freedom of expression*
>
> *b. the extent to which it is in the public interest for the material to be published, while at the same time keeping in mind any relevant issue of privacy.*

The media's right to freedom of expression is an important part of the injunction debate but the court must also consider 'any relevant privacy code'.

This means that the court will look to see if newspaper journalists have behaved in accordance with the Press Complaints Commission's code of conduct or broadcast journalists with the Ofcom code.

The judge also takes into account the extent to which the information is already in the public domain and also the extent of public interest in its disclosure.

If an injunction is granted, it applies not only to the newspaper directly concerned but to all other media organisations who know about the injunction.

DANGER OF PRIOR RESTRAINT

Following Max Mosley's successful action against the News of the World he complained that the story had been published without warning. He had not been given the chance to apply for an injunction to prevent publication of a story which caused immense distress to himself, his wife, who had previously known nothing about his S&M sessions, and the rest of his family.

This is a key issue in privacy cases. Because there had been a run of public figures gagging newspapers by successfully applying for injunctions prior to publication, the News of the World chose not to put the allegations to Mosley before publication. Mosley was later campaigning to get a change in the law to compel the media to inform 'victims' prior to publication of confidential information.

Desmond Browne QC, the chairman of the Bar Council, was referring to Mosley's campaign when he said: "If newspapers are going to intrude on privacy without giving notice, they ought only to do so at peril of being milked for exemplary damages."

This idea - restraining the media prior to publication - goes against the media's freedom of expression. At present, if they get it wrong they pay the price afterwards through libel or privacy actions. The damages in the Mosley case amounted to £60,000. The legal costs to about £1,000,000.

Prior restraint would also be to the detriment of investigative journalism. Even in the Reynolds defence check-list for responsible journalism *(see Libel: common law privilege)* it is recognised that sometimes it is impracticable to put the evidence to the subject of the story in advance because that gives the corrupt the chance to fabricate a cover-up.

The code for public interest

One of the first things to remember about the 'public interest' is that the courts will only grant that defence after checking that the journalists have conformed to the appropriate code of conduct.

The courts are bound to do that under the terms of the Human Rights Act.

The code for print journalists it is the Editors' Code of Practice which is adjudicated on by the Press Complaints Commission. For broadcast journalists it is the code adjudicated by Ofcom and the BBC also has a set of guidelines for its journalists.

In straightforward terms 'the public interest' is best defined as in the PCC code:

1. Detecting or exposing crime or serious impropriety

2. Protecting public health and safety.

3. Protecting the public from being misled by the actions or statements of individuals or organisations.

When the News of the World claimed public interest in the Mosley case they said they were exposing serious impropriety (as in no.1 above).

When The Mirror defended its exposure of Naomi Campbell's drug addiction it was on the grounds of protecting the public from the model's earlier statements that she did not take drugs (no.3 above).

Public interest becomes less straightforward in privacy cases because here there are two 'public interests' in competition with each other.

1. Public interest in providing protection for confidential information.

2. Public interest in the public receiving the kind of information which is necessary for them to make choices as members of a democratic society.

So as a general rule the courts will give 'public interest' protection to stories which affect the daily life of the general population as outlined in the PCC code above.

But privacy case law indicates more and more clearly that the courts will not see a public interest defence in stories about celebrity sex life – no matter how interesting the public find them. It is a case of the public interest not what the public finds interesting.

The test according to the Strasbourg court in the Princess Caroline case *(Von Hannover v Germany)* is: Would the information (the story or picture) make a contribution to "a debate of general interest"?

The House of Lords interpreted that as meaning that generally speaking "political speech" would be accorded greater value than gossip or "tittle-tattle".

The code for public interest

In Mosley v News Group Mr Justice Eady made the following observations about the type of personal information the disclosure of which would <u>not</u> be in the public interest,

* First, it is said that it is legitimate sometimes to infringe an individual's privacy for the greater good of exposing or detecting crime. The question has to be asked whether it will always be an automatic defence to intrusive journalism that a crime was being committed on private property, however technical or trivial? Would it justify installing a camera in someone's home, for example, in order to catch him or her smoking a spliff? Surely not. There must be some limits and, even in more serious cases, any such intrusion should be no more than is proportionate.

* The modern approach to personal privacy and to sexual preferences and practices is very different from that of past generations. First, there is a greater willingness, and especially in the Strasbourg jurisprudence, to accord respect to an individual's right to conduct his or her personal life without state interference or condemnation.

* It has now to be recognised that sexual conduct is a significant aspect of human life in respect of which people should be free to choose. That freedom is one of the matters which Article 8 protects.

* It is not for the state or for the media to expose sexual conduct which does not involve any significant breach of the criminal law. That is so whether the motive for such intrusion is merely prurience or a moral crusade.

* It is not simply a matter of personal privacy versus the public interest. The modern perception is that there is a public interest in respecting personal privacy.

* Anyone indulging in sexual activity is entitled to a degree of privacy – especially if it is on private property and between consenting adults (paid or unpaid).

* Sexual activity engages the privacy rights protected by Article 8 because it concerns a most intimate aspect of private life.

* People's sex lives are to be regarded as essentially their own business – provided at least that the participants are genuinely consenting adults and there is no question of exploiting the young or vulnerable.

* Public figures are entitled to a private personal life. The notion of privacy covers not only sexual activities but personal relationships more generally. That again states the position according to the ruling in Von Hannover v Germany.

The two types of confidence

The first is still termed Breach of Confidence.
The second is known as Misuse of Private Information.

We have seen how the introduction of the Human Rights Act in 2000 led immediately to a widening of the existing English law of confidence and how that law continued to be the cornerstone upon which 'privacy' cases were decided.

The confidence referred to in the phrase 'breach of confidence' was the confidence arising out of a confidential relationship. This law imposes a "duty of confidence" on a person who receives information they know is reasonably to be regarded as confidential.

Before the law was expanded there were rules about when information should be considered confidential and breach of confidence claims still depended on there being a pre-existing confidential relationship (doctor/patient, lawyer/client etc) between the informant and the victim.

There was no general protection for information which fell outside those rules but which people would still prefer to keep private. Many media stories emanated from sources that had no pre-existing relationship with the victim yet the information disclosed was still of a private nature.

Case law since the introduction of the Human Rights Act had expanded the law of confidence to take account of both article 8 (respect for private and family life) and the competing article 10 (freedom of expression).

The significant expansion to solve the 'pre-existing relationship' problem was made in the Naomi Campbell v Mirror case with the formulation of what is now known as 'misuse of private information.'

Say a journalist found a file containing newsworthy information on a train. That information could not be regarded as 'confidential' because the journalist did not owe any obligation of confidence to the owner. But the information was certainly private and under the new rules the journalist, if he published, might be sued for misuse of that private information.

We will next examine breach of confidence and misuse of private information in detail.

Breach of confidence

An action for breach of confidence takes place after someone reveals information - usually to the media - which, it is argued by the 'victim', had been given them in confidence and which they were obliged to keep secret.

That confidentiality can be either explicit or implicit. An *explicit* duty of confidence concerns people who have expressly agreed to keep information confidential, usually by written contract. An *implicit* duty means that the nature of the information and circumstances under which it was gathered imply that a person should keep the information confidential.

There is a three-point test for 'old-fashioned' breach of confidence

1. The information must have ' the necessary quality of confidence.'

What is the 'necessary quality'? The test for this was given in the *Naomi Campbell* case by Lord Hope: " The underlying question is whether the information that was disclosed was private and not public. If the information is obviously private, the situation will be one where the person to whom it relates can reasonably expect his privacy to be respected."

Information held by the courts to be 'obviously private' includes trade secrets, the plot of a Harry Potter book, details of people's sex lives, medical treatments, diaries, a company's business plans – none of them trivial matters. The law will not protect trivia.

2. The information must have been imparted in circumstances imposing an obligation of confidence.

This is all about the nature of relationships. An obligation of confidence arises when information is obtained in circumstances where the person obtaining it realised that it was intended to be kept confidential. Obvious circumstances are when information is passed between doctor and patient, lawyer and client, priest and penitent and man and wife.

Since 2000 courts have recognised that there are personal relationships outside conventional marriage which need to be protected but have made clear that the more casual the relationship the less likely that revelations about it will be protected.

The Blackburn Rovers player Gary Flitcroft and the television presenter Jamie Theakston both failed to keep their indiscretions out of the papers because of this relationship issue.

Theakston (right) tried to suppress a story about his visit to a Mayfair brothel but the court refused to grant a gagging injunction because the relationship between prostitute and client was too transitory to be protected by confidentiality. In Flitcroft's case it was extra-marital affairs with two women, one for three months, the other for a year. The court decided that such transient affairs could not carry the same confidentiality as that between married couples or long-term partners.

In the Mosley case it was argued not only that the content of the published material was inherently private in nature but that there had also been a pre-existing relationship of confidentiality between the participants.

They had all known each other for some time and took part in such activities on the understanding that they would be private and that none of them would reveal what had taken place. It was an unwritten rule among them that people were trusted not to reveal what had gone on.

The woman who sold the story was held to have breached that trust and it was noted that the journalist concerned must have appreciated that she was doing so because he supplied her with a concealed camera and instructed her how to use it without her being suspected by her fellow participants.

An obligation of confidence can also arise in the following situations:

Employment Contracts

Many people have a clause in their employment contracts banning them from exploiting information they obtained as a result of their work - nannies and PAs employed by celebrities are an obvious example. But even if there is no specific confidentiality clause there is an implied term in every contract that the employee will not act in any way detrimental to his employer's interests. There are exceptions to that implied duty of confidence. In *Tillery Valley Foods v Channel 4* a television journalist took a job at a factory and secretly filmed procedures which were unhygienic. The company sought an injunction on the grounds that the information was obtained in breach of employer-employee confidence. The injunction was refused.

Government employees

Members of the security services, civil servants, members of the armed forces – none of them have written employment contracts but the courts have determined, notably in the Peter Wright *Spycatcher* case, that they have a duty of confidence with regard to information obtained through their work.

The media

In most cases the media is the third party in a breach of confidence claim. It is the relationship between the informer and the victim which creates the obligation of confidence but once that obligation exists it covers anyone else who makes unauthorised use of the information - providing they know it was obtained as a result of a breach of confidence.

Misuse of private information

This is when the balancing act between articles 8 and 10 takes place.

The court has to decide two points:

> 1. Did the claimant have a reasonable expectation of privacy with respect to the information disclosed?
>
> *If so*
>
> 2. Was the person's right to privacy more important, in the circumstances, than someone else's right to freedom of expression?

1. Reasonable expectation of privacy

The question the courts ask is a simple one: Was the information obviously private?

Where the answer to the question is not 'obvious' then Lord Hope, in the *Campbell* case, suggested that the test should be whether or not the information disclosed would give substantial offence to the victim. The mind that had to be examined was not that of any ordinary reader of the information but of the person affected by the publicity.

Lord Hope referred to pictures taken of Campbell outside a hall in London where the Narcotics Anonymous meetings where held. The pictures were taken on a public street and so were not 'obviously' private, neither did they show her in an embarrassing light to the ordinary reader. Therefore the court had to consider what their effect would be on someone in her position. As she was a recovering drug addict she would be vulnerable and the publication of the pictures might well adversely affect her treatment. This, said Lord Hope, suggested that Campbell had a legitimate expectation of privacy and the pictures should not have been used.

In the Mosley case, the News of the World claimed that Mosley had no reasonable expectation of privacy in relation to the S&M orgy or in relation to the pictures in the newspaper. The paper's lawyers argued that Mosley's right to privacy under article 8 was outweighed by a greater public interest in disclosure because of Mosley's role as president of the FIA and the newspaper's right to freedom of expression under article 10 should prevail.

Mr Justice Eady said that when the courts identified an infringement of a person's rights under article 8, and in particular his freedom to conduct his sex life and personal relationships as he wishes, it was right for the courts to provide that person with a remedy. The only permitted exception was where there was a countervailing public interest which was strong enough to outweigh it.

He had to examine, therefore, whether it had been necessary and proportionate for the intrusion to take place, for example, in order to expose illegal activity or to prevent the public from being significantly misled by public claims made by the individual concerned (as with Naomi Campbell's public denials of drug-taking)?

Or was the intrusion necessary because the information, in the words of the Strasbourg court in *Von Hannover,* would make a contribution to "a debate of general interest"? Eady said there could be little doubt that intimate photographs or recording of private sexual activity, however unconventional, would be extremely difficult to justify at all by Strasbourg standards.

Titillation for its own sake could never be justified. Yet it was reasonable to suppose that it was titillation which led 30,000 people to accept the News of the World's invitation to "see the shocking video at notw.co.uk".

It would be quite unrealistic to think that these visits were prompted by a desire to participate in a "debate of general interest" of the kind contemplated in *Von Hannover.* Mr Justice Eady, therefore, ruled that Mosley plainly had a reasonable expectation of privacy.

2. The balancing test: privacy versus freedom of expression

If the first hurdle can be overcome, by demonstrating a reasonable expectation of privacy, the court is required to carry out the next step of weighing the competing rights of art.8 and art.10 in the light of an "intense focus" upon the individual facts of the case.

No one right takes automatic precedence over another. The right of free expression is no longer regarded as being superior to any privacy rights that may be established on the part of the claimant. The court's approach of applying an intense focus to individual cases means that the old justifications like "public figures must expect to have less privacy" or "people in positions of responsibility must be role models" no longer carry any weight.

In *Campbell,* the House of Lords said that the ultimate balancing test has been recognised as turning to a large extent upon proportionality. Was the intrusion into the claimant's privacy proportionate to the public interest supposedly being served by it? In other words had the media gone over the top in the way the story was presented.

This legal theory of presenting the story in a manner proportionate to its public interest value can be illustrated by the way the News of the World covered the Mosley exposure.

Here are the captions to some of the pictures the newspaper used when it revealed Mosley's S&M session with five prostitutes.

> i) "FASTEST SLAP Racing boss Mosley wallops one of the squealing hookers with leather paddle."
>
> ii) "SO SICK In the midst of one beating, a panting Mosley watches one hooker take off her Nazi uniform."

iii) "IN CHAINS Mosley lies face down on a bed trussed up before his punishment."

iv) "TAKE ZAT! Formula One supremo Mosley is bent naked and chained over the torture bench in the S&M dungeon as one of the hookers lays into his bare buttocks so hard with a cane he needed a dressing to cover the wounds."

v) "SINISTER Hooker in mock death-camp clothes is gagged."

vi) "TEA-TIME: Mosley after orgy."

vii) "TWISTED GAME: Hooker ticks off SS-style inspection sheet. Mosley has called himself 'Tim Barnes' to earn extra punishment."

The question Mr Justice Eady had to decide was whether the pictures were necessary in the public interest as a means of revealing any wrong-doing on the part of Mosley and the five women. Whether, in fact, the coverage was out of proportion to the extent the orgy mattered in the great scheme of things. Was it necessary to heap such humiliation on the participants?

The legal principles involved were stated in Strasbourg in the case of *Leempoel v Belgium, 2006:* " When striking a balance between protecting private life and freedom of expression the Court has always emphasised the requirement that the publication should serve the public interest and make a contribution to a debate of general interest.

" While the right for the public to be informed may even relate to aspects of the private life of public persons, publications whose sole aim is to satisfy the curiosity of a certain public as to the details of the private life of a person, whatever their fame, should not be regarded as contributing to any debate of general interest to society."

In the light of that judgment the question for Mr Justice Eady would be: Were S&M orgies a topic of discussion and concern to the public at large? If the answer was 'Yes' there would be a public interest in providing the information. If the answer was 'No' the story served only to titillate .

The guideline about pictures in particular is contained in the case of *Douglas v Hello! Ltd* when the Court of Appeal said that special considerations attach to photographs, which enabled the person viewing the photograph to act as a spectator, in some circumstances, as a voyeur.

The courts had also to take into account the manner in which the pictures were taken. The pictures of Mosley had been taken by with a hidden camera activated by one of the prostitutes.

Eady referred to the Press Complaints Commission code of conduct when he discussed the ethics of that operation:

> i) The press must not seek to obtain or publish material acquired by using hidden cameras or clandestine listening devices; or by intercepting private or mobile telephone calls, messages or emails; or by the unauthorised removal of documents or photographs or by accessing digitally-held private information without consent.

> ii) Engaging in misrepresentation or subterfuge, including by agents or intermediaries, can generally be justified only in the public interest and then only when the material cannot be obtained by other means.

Eady concluded that the very fact of clandestine recording could be regarded as an intrusion and an unacceptable infringement of article 8 rights.

The nature and scale of the distress caused by the Mosley story was in large measure due to the clandestine filming and the pictures acquired as a result.

Lord Hoffmann in *Campbell*, summed up the proportionality question. He said there could be a genuine public interest in the disclosure of the existence of a sexual relationship but warned that the addition of salacious details or intimate photographs would be disproportionate and unacceptable. "They would", he said, " be too intrusive and demeaning".

Press Complaints Commission

One of the effects of the Human Rights Act has been to widen the Press Complaints Commission's view of what is, and what is not, private.

In 2000, Anna Ford complained that OK! magazine and the Daily Mail had invaded her privacy by publishing pictures of her on a beach. At that time the PCC decided she had no right to privacy because the beach was open to the public.

Nine years later, following an identical complaint by the England manager Fabio Capello, the PCC presided over an agreement which saw the Daily Mail and the News of the World apologising and paying substantial amounts to charity for invading the privacy of Capello and his wife who were photographed on a Spanish beach having had a mud bath.

This change of tack by the PCC followed the European Court of Human Rights decision in *Von Hannover v Germany* which formulated the principle that the key question when balancing (the Capellos') right of privacy and (the newspapers') right to freedom of expression was to what extent did the published material contribute to a 'debate of general interest.'

In the Hannover case the court said that pictures of Princess Caroline shopping with her children made no contribution to any debate of general interest. There was no legitimate public interest in seeing pictures of the princess when she was not performing her official duties. She had a legitimate expectation of privacy for her private life - even in public places.

The PCC's code on privacy is an acknowledgment of that decision. It reads:

i) Everyone is entitled to respect for his or her private and family life, home, health and correspondence, including digital communications. Editors will be expected to justify intrusions into any individual's private life without consent.

ii) It is unacceptable to photograph individuals in a private place without their consent. *Note - private places are public or private property where there is a reasonable expectation of privacy.*

Pictures can be trade secrets

OK! then - but no more than a glimpse

The 2003 High Court case of *Michael Douglas and Catherine Zeta Jones v Hello!* decided that the right of celebrities to sell pictures of themselves was the equivalent of a trade secret and was therefore protected by the law of confidentiality.

Guests at the wedding of Douglas and Zeta Jones were forbidden to take pictures after the couple sold exclusive rights to OK! magazine. But a paparazzo smuggled himself in, secretly photographed the bride and groom, and sold the shots to OK's rival Hello!

The court had to balance the rights of the Douglases - the confidentiality of the information in the pictures - against Hello's right to freedom of expression and the public's right to know about the wedding.

Mr Justice Lyndsey's decision that the wedding was a private event was the cornerstone of the success of their claim for breach of confidence.

The fact that the couple had previously welcomed publicity at other events did not lessen their right to complain about the intrusion into their private wedding and the financial consequences of that intrusion. The judge said that information about some people's private lives had become a highly lucrative commodity for some sections of the media.

Protection was to be given to public figures against such intrusion although people in public life had to expect greater scrutiny than others.

The judge analysed the right of confidence enjoyed by the couple as a hybrid variety involving personal and commercial confidence. He relied on concepts familiar in trade secrets cases in finding that the Douglases' rights in confidence had been breached as had those of OK!.

The finding was based on the Douglases having a valuable commercial commodity (the pictures) the value of which depended upon its content at first being kept secret and then being made public in ways controlled by the couple.

Protecting the right to life

There are some cases in which the courts have used the law of confidence to protect the identity of people in accordance with their right to life and their right not to be tortured as guaranteed by the Human Rights Act.

IN 2000 an injunction was granted giving the the killers of James Bulger a life-time anonymity prior to their release from prison. The injunction, which was opposed by three newspaper groups, followed threats by Ralph Bulger, the father of the murdered boy, that he would hunt Jon Venables and Robert Thompson down.

Dame Elizabeth Butler-Sloss, president of the Family Division of the High Court, granting the injunction to prevent their whereabouts being known, said: "Under the umbrella of confidentiality there will be information which may require a special quality of protection."

The disclosure of Venables and Thompson's whereabouts would have infringed three rights under the Human Rights Act – their right to life, their right not to be tortured and their right to privacy.

This identity screen was maintained when, in July 2010, Venables pleaded guilty by video link to downloading and distributing indecent images of children, and was jailed for two years. The Old Bailey case was conducted via a link to the undisclosed prison where Venables had been held since his arrest. The screen in front of the presiding judge, Mr Justice Bean, was set at such an angle that he alone could see Venable's face, all that those in the court could hear was Venable's disembodied voice.

Earlier, lawyers for the media asked if the rest of the court could see the screen. They argued it was a very serious departure from the principle of open justice and the first time such steps had ever been taken for an adult criminal defendant. But the judge refused their request, saying the risk of Venables being identified and later attacked justified the decision.

The judge partially lifted reporting restrictions to reveal Venables had been living in Cheshire at the time of the offences and that the case was dealt with by Cheshire police and Cheshire probation service. It was also revealed that Cheshire police had produced a threat assessment to try to establish what could happen to Venables were his assumed identity revealed. It concluded that Venables would face the highest possible risk of being attacked if his new name was either published in the media or known elsewhere in society. The threat assessment document said "someone could find Venables with the intention of killing him".

In 2003 Dame Elizabeth Butler-Sloss granted child-killer Mary Bell and her teenage daughter an injunction which similarly guarantees them anonymity for life. Dame Butler-Sloss made the order forbidding disclosure of the identities and whereabouts of the two women to protect their right to private and family life under article 8. Dame Elizabeth said that she was satisfied that Bell's fragile mental state and other factors, such as her age (10) at the time of the killings, justified the interference with the right to free expression under art.10. She accepted evidence that mother and daughter were at considerable risk of press intrusion and harassment and public stigma if their identities were disclosed. They had been forced by press intrusion to relocate five times and to change identities three times. Dame Elizabeth said the media had not opposed the injunction and the attorney general and the official solicitor supported it.

IN 2004 The High Court banned the media from publishing any information about Maxine Carr, the girlfriend of Ian Huntley who murdered the two Soham school girls. Carr had been released from prison after serving a sentence for providing Huntley with a false alibi. Earlier she had received death threats and was given a new identity but reporters still traced her. Carr immediately went to court and obtained an injunction which forbids the media from publishing any information about her new identity or whereabouts and, even more, forbids any attempts to find out such information.

THE CASE of *Ellis v Chief Constable of Essex (2003)* has wider implications for the media. The claimant, Gary Ellis, 27, had numerous convictions for offences of dishonesty and car-related crime. Essex Police proposed to "name and shame" him in a picture-poster campaign as a means of reducing burglary and car crime. Ellis claimed that this would involve interference with his, his parents, his ex-partner and his child's right to respect for private and family life. The High Court found that any name-and-shame scheme needed appraisal before a decision could be taken as to whether its possible benefits were proportionate to the intrusion into an offender's right to respect for his private and family life. In considering the selection of an offender for such a scheme it would be important to bear in mind that the offender's family, and in particular any children, also had rights to respect for their privacy and family life.

Campbell 4 - The Mirror 5 (and The Mirror loses)

Not acceptable - the street was public but the occasion was private

The pictures were grainy but clear enough to show a distressed Naomi Campbell surrounded by friends in the street outside the hall where she had been attending a meeting of Narcotics Anonymous. The pictures and the information about Campbell's attempts to beat a drug addiction were central to the privacy case Campbell launched against The Mirror.

It started in the High Court where she won, went on to the Court of Appeal where she lost and finished up in the House of Lords where she won on a split verdict 3-2.

In all, nine of the finest legal minds in the land took part in the three stages of the adjudication. Five of them agreed with The Mirror, four of them with Campbell.

But three of the four formed the majority in the supreme court, the Lords, and Campbell prevailed in a landmark case which finally established that the UK had a law capable of protecting 'private' as well as 'confidential' information. In everything but name, a Law of Privacy.

The Mirror broke the story in February 2001, claiming that Campbell was attending the self-help group to help cure her drug addiction. The story led to a prolonged legal battle, the three stages of which are analysed below:

THE HIGH COURT: Campbell sued the newspaper, claiming that the report amounted to a breach of confidence and a violation of both the Human Rights Act and the Data Protection Act. The High Court accepted her arguments and ordered the Mirror to pay damages of £3,500. The newspaper appealed.

Acceptable - putting the record straight

THE COURT OF APPEAL: In October 2002, three Appeal Court judges overturned the High Court decision, ordering her to repay the damages and to pay the Mirror's £350,000 costs. They reasoned that the report was in the public interest, because Campbell had previously publicly denied taking drugs.

Lord Phillips had ruled that, where a public figure chose to make untrue pronouncements about his or her private life, the press would normally be entitled to put the record straight.

The Appeal Court also found that the journalist had to be given reasonable latitude as to the manner in which the story was conveyed to the public or else his right to freedom of expression under the European Convention on Human Rights would be "unnecessarily inhibited."

THE HOUSE OF LORDS: Campbell's appeal to the House of Lords neither argued that the Mirror was wrong to report the fact that she had used drugs, nor to report that she was receiving treatment for her addiction.

Instead, her complaint was that the newspaper breached her confidence and invaded her privacy when it published details of her treatment, including the frequency of her attendance at therapy sessions. She argued that therapy was essentially private and that there had been a breach of confidence by an unknown source who tipped off the Mirror.

Campbell claimed that the existing law of confidence could be used to protect privacy and that this could be balanced with the law on freedom of expression. The Mirror claimed there was no such law of privacy.

The House of Lords agreed with Campbell. English law did protect privacy and a major impetus for this had been the Human Rights Act 1998, which enshrined the European Convention on Human Rights into English law.

The law of confidence is (in the words of dissenting judge Lord Nicholls) "better encapsulated now as a misuse of private information".

He parted company from three of his fellow judges on the facts, but none disagreed with his analysis of the law. All the judges agreed that information relating to drug addiction and treatment should be regarded as private information and attracts the protection of article 8.

It was also common ground between Campbell and the Mirror that the newspaper was entitled to report the fact of Campbell's drug addition and the fact she was receiving treatment for it because she had publicly denied she used drugs and the Mirror was entitled to correct the position.

The key question in the action was whether the Mirror was entitled to go on to give details of Campbell's treatment and to publish a photograph of her leaving the clinic. In a 3:2 majority, the House of Lords decided that it was not so entitled: the publication of additional information relating to the fact that Campbell was receiving treatment at Narcotics

Anonymous, details of that treatment and a photograph of her leaving the clinic was not necessary or justified and did infringe her privacy.

Accordingly they revised the verdict of the Court of Appeal and reinstated the trial verdict in the High Court in favour of Campbell.

The majority judges concluded that while, in the words of Baroness Hale, "not every statement about a person's health will carry the badge of confidentiality" (she gave the example of a broken leg) there was a real risk that a report in a newspaper about treatment for drug addiction could do great harm. Recovering drug addicts were bound to be in a fragile state.

The majority judges also attached significant weight to the publication of the photograph. Lord Hope said that " had it not been for the publication of the photographs ...I would have been inclined to regard the balance (between art.8 and art.10 rights) as about even." The photographs had added greatly to the intrusion.

So there we have it. We do have a law of privacy and the media cannot afford to ignore it. They need to be particularly careful if they are thinking of illustrating an article with an intrusive photograph taken without the subject's consent or of publishing significant detail about someone's private life even if some of the information may be considered to be in the public interest.

Significantly the House of Lords recognised that everyone is entitled to respect for their privacy and this can extend to pictures taken of them in a public street.

Credit: This case study is largely taken from a report on the House of Lords decision written by Claire Gill, a partner in the London law firm of Carter-Ruck and is used with her permission.

THE END
How The Mirror summed it all up.

Landmark privacy cases

2008: Protection for children of celebrities

David Murray, aged five, followed Naomi Campbell in adding another building block to privacy laws. The son of the Harry Potter author JK Rowling , won a landmark Court of Appeal ruling establishing that the law protects the children of celebrities from the publication of unauthorised photographs, unless their parents have exposed them to publicity.

Rowling and her husband Dr Neil Murray brought the case in their son's name in an attempt to ban publication of long-lens pictures of the boy taken when he was 19-months-old by an agency photographer. In one picture, published in the Sunday Express, David was being pushed in a buggy by his parents near their home in Edinburgh.

Express Newspapers settled the case against it for invasion of privacy out of court but the agency, Big Pictures, applied to the High Court to have the claim against it struck out and were succesful. Mr Justice Patten rejected the parents' claim, saying that "the law does not in my judgment (as it stands) allow them to carve out a press-free zone for their children in respect of absolutely everything".

But three Appeal Court judges, headed by the Master of the Rolls, Sir Anthony Clarke, overturned that judgment. Clarke, England's second most senior judge, said : "If a child of parents who are not in the public eye could reasonably expect not to have photographs of him published in the media, so too should the child of a famous parent."

2005: Protection for confidences told to friends

McKennitt v Ash: Ms McKennitt, a Canadian folk singer, fell out with her long-time travelling companion and close friend Ms Ash who later wrote a book in which she revealed details of Mc Kennitt's personal and sexual relationships as well as many details about the singer's emotional vulnerablity. The High Court said that the details were only available to Ms Ash because of the close friendship and Ms McKennitt had a reasonable expectation that conversations between them would remain private. The decision was later upheld by the Court of Appeal.

2004: Protection for public figures - even in public places.

In *Von Hannover v Germany* at the European Court of Human Rights, Princess Caroline of Monaco complained that paparazzi were continually following her as she went about normal daily activities like taking her children to school.

The German courts found against her on the basis that the public had a right to know about the ordinary daily life of a public figure. The European court disagreed and formulated the principle that the key question when balancing the rights of privacy and freedom of expression was to what extent did the published material contribute to a 'debate of general interest.'

In the case of Princess Caroline the pictures made no contribution to any debate of general interest. There was no legitimate public interest in seeing pictures of the princess when she was not perfoming her official duties. She had a legitimate expectation of privacy for her private life - even in public places.

Sienna Miller victory may clip paparazzi's wings

David Brown

'It may well encourage others followed in such a way to take action'

Sienna Miller's success in winning £53,000 damages from paparazzi photographers in a landmark action using anti-harassment laws has had important repercussions for celebrities and the picture agencies who pursue them.

The star had sued the London-based Big Pictures agency claiming that her life had been made intolerable by photographers invading her privacy and pursuing her across the world. In addition to paying damages and costs the agency also agreed not to photograph Miller at her home or to pursue her for pictures.

The action was the first time a celebrity had succesfully sued photographers using anti-harassment law designed to curb the activities of stalkers. Miller's example was followed by Amy Winehouse and Lily Allen.

The celebrities have followed the example set in 2001 by a civilian police station clerk, Esther Thomas, who sued The Sun after the paper had reported her complaint against four officers over their behaviour when a Somali asylum-seeker sought help.

The Sun described Ms Thomas as a 'black clerk', and said her complaint led to the demotion of two sergeants and a £700 fine for a constable. The paper quoted a "fellow cop" as saying: "It was essentially light-hearted banter in private and the Somali never heard. This is political correctness gone mad."

The following week the paper published a selection of readers letters attacking Ms Thomas for making the complaint and ruining the sergeants' careers. This was followed by a story seeking readers' contributions to pay the pc's fine. In the meantime, Ms Thomas received race hate mail.

The Sun tried to have the claim struck out but the Court of Appeal held that Ms Thomas had an arguable case. Where harassment involved publication it might be held that to cause someone distress was an abuse of the freedom of the press.

The Protection Against Harassment Act 1997 makes it a crime to pursue a course of conduct which alarms the victim or causes them distress. It could include door-stepping, repeated phone calls or - as in Sienna Miller's case - pursuit by paparazzi.

Data Protection

Besides her privacy claim, Naomi Campbell had also sued the Mirror under the Data Protection Act 1998 (DTA). The point at issue was whether the information revealed by the newspaper was 'sensitive personal data' and, if it was, was the Mirror entitled to publish it.

The House of Lords did not go on to consider data protection issues after they ruled in favour of Ms Campbell over the misuse of private information. But the issue was considered in both the High Court and the Court of Appeal. In the High Court, Mr Justice Morland awarded £3,500 damages to Campbell for both breach of confidence and contravention of the Data Protection Act 1998.

On the Data Protection Act, the judge said that the information contained in the Mirror article as to the nature of, and details of, the therapy that Campbell was receiving, including the photographs with captions, was clearly related to her physical or mental health or condition and was therefore "sensitive personal data" as defined by the Act.

He ruled that the Mirror did not have one of the legitimising conditions in the Act to enable it to lawfully publish such material. Those conditions are:

> "The data controller (the newspaper in this case) believes, having regard to the importance of freedom of expression, that publication would be in the public interest and

> "The data controller reasonably believes that not to process the information would be incompatible with journalism."

The Court of Appeal overturned that judgement on the data protection. Lord Phillips ruled that, where a public figure chose to make untrue pronouncements about his or her private life, the press would normally be entitled to put the record straight.

Therefore, a journalism exemption in the Data Protection Act applied, and the newspaper was entitled to publish the report in the public interest.

The court reasoned that the story would not carry credibility without sufficient detail.

" The detail given, and indeed the photographs, were a legitimate, if not an essential, part of the journalistic package designed to demonstrate that Miss Campbell had been deceiving the public when she said she did not take drugs.

"Given that is was legitimate for the [newspaper] to publish the fact she was a drug addict and receiving treatment, it does not seem it was particularly significant to add the fact the treatment consisted of attendance at meetings of Narcotics Anonymous."

It can be seen, therefore, that issues of data protection and the media will always end up with a subjective argument centred on public interest. Like breach of confidence and misuse of private information the outcome of cases will be difficult to forecast.

Personal data

The Data Protection Act 1998 (DPA) recognizes an individual's rights to privacy in a world where vast amounts of personal information are held on computers and in manual files.

The Act helps protect an *individual* from having personal information misused. Information about companies is not subject to the DPA unless named individuals are referred to as a point of contact.

The personal data gets protection only if it is stored in either computers or manual filing systems. There are two categories of data.

Personal data is information that can identify a person by itself or in combination with another source in the possession of the data controller. It also includes any expression of opinion about the individual.

Personal data is not restricted to private information such as medical records or financial details. Under the DPA it could include information, such as a magazine subscription list, which is processed automatically.

A person's favourite television programmes or his shopping habits comes under the DPA if that information, linked with other information held by the television company or the supermarket, can lead to the identification of the particular individual.

Sensitive personal data consists of personal data relating to a person's :

* Racial or ethnic origin.
* Political views.
* Religious beliefs or beliefs of a similar nature.
* Membership of a trade union.
* Physical or mental health or condition.
* Sexual life.
* Encounters with the law.

Individual rights

The person or organisation holding the information – the Data Controller – must obtain and use the personal data in accordance with the data protection principles listed in the DPA.

These are:

1. Personal data must be processed in a fair and lawful manner and processing will be unlawful unless at least one of the following conditions are met:

* The subject of the personal data has given his consent to the processing.

* The processing is necessary to perform a contract.

* The processing is necessary to comply with a legal obligation or the administration of justice or for the exercise of any functions conferred under any enactment. For the exercise of any functions of the crown, a minister of the crown, or a government department, or for the exercise of any other functions of a public nature exercised in the public interest by any person.

* To protect the vital interests of the subject of the personal data.

2. Personal data shall be obtained only for specified and lawful purposes.

3. Personal data shall be adequate, relevant and not excessive in relation for the purpose for which it is processed.

4. Personal data must be accurate and kept up to date.

5. Personal data should not be kept for longer than necessary.

6. Personal data should be processed in accordance with the rights of data subjects under the DPA. The individual is entitled to:

* Find out from the data controller if any personal data is being processed.

* Ask the data controller to stop processing the information if it is causing or likely to cause him substantial damage or distress.

* Apply to the courts to rectify, block, erase or destroy personal data.

* An absolute right that the data should not be used for the purposes of direct marketing to him.

* A right to ensure that no decision is taken that significantly affects the individual based solely on automatic processing, for example his creditworthiness.

* A right to compensation from the data controller if the individual suffers loss for any contravention of the DPA and compensation also for any distress caused.

Processing data

Personal data must be processed in a fair and lawful manner.

Processing will be unlawful unless at least one of the following conditions are met:

* The subject of the personal data has given his consent to the processing.

* The processing is necessary to perform a contract.

* The processing is necessary to comply with a legal obligation or the administration of justice or for the exercise of any functions conferred under any enactment.

* For the exercise of any functions of the crown, a minister of the crown, or a government department, or for the exercise of any other functions of a public nature exercised in the public interest by any person.

* To protect the vital interests of the subject of the personal data.

Sensitive Personal data can be processed only if two conditions are met – one of them from the list above and the second from (among others contained in Schedule 3) the following:

* The person gave explicit consent or

* The processing is necessary under employment legislation.

* The processing is necessary in order to protect the vital interests of the data subject or another person (usually relied on by the data controller if consent cannot be given by or on behalf of the subject of the personal data).

* The processing is carried out in the course of legitimate activities by a non-profit political, philosophical, religious or trade union body or organisation in relation to members of the body or those connected with it.

* The information has been made public as a result of steps deliberately taken by the subject of the personal data.

* The processing is necessary in connection with legal proceedings, legal advice or legal rights.

* The processing is necessary for the administration of justice.

* The processing is necessary for medical purposes.

* The processing is of sensitive personal data consisting of information relating to racial or ethnic origin necessary for identifying equality of opportunity or treatment.

Exemptions for the media

The processing of personal data that concern journalism is not affected by the DPA if all of the following apply:

The processing is undertaken with a view to the publication of journalistic material.

The data controller believes, having regard to the importance of freedom of expression, that publication would be in the public interest and

The data controller reasonably believes that not to process the information would be incompatible with journalism.

An example of when the exemption might apply is the use of details of the previous convictions of a farmer in a television documentary about vets who investigate cruelty to animals.

Since the passing of the DPA the Government has bowed to media pressure by issuing a statutory instrument which sets out circumstances in which sensitive personal data may be processed in the 'substantial public interest'. They include:

Disclosures for journalistic purposes of personal data relating to:

The commission by any person of any unlawful act, whether alleged or established.

Dishonesty, malpractice or other seriously improper conduct by, or the unfitness or incompetence of, any person, whether alleged or established.

Mismanagement in the administration of, or failures in services provided by, any body or association, whether alleged or established.

Processing information for the prevention or detection of any unlawful act where seeking the consent of the data subject to the processing would prejudice those purposes.

Processing which has the function of protecting members of the public from certain conduct which may constitute an unlawful act, such as incompetence or mismanagement.

THE RIGHT TO KNOW

1. The Freedom of Information (FOI) Act
2. The Environmental Information Regulations

The Independent's splash was a story which would probably never have seen the light of day if the Freedom on Information Act had not come into being in January 2005.

Even then, the paper had to battle for three years to obtain details of more than 100 letters and memos written by ministers and members of the Royal Household during negotiations over public subsidies for the upkeep of the Queen's palaces.

In the end, the Information Commission ruled that under the Freedom of Information Act the public interest in releasing the letters and other documents outweighed the Royal Family's right to protection - a further indication that the Act has radically changed Britain's climate of secrecy for the better.

It also illustrated the fact that sometimes information can be withheld for up to three or four years in a laborious appeals process which has left the Information Commission office swamped with cases. A CFOI study revealed that of 493 cases still outstanding in the 18 months to March 2008, 46 per cent had been delayed by between one and two years, 25per cent by between two and three years and five per cent by more than three years.

Politicians and civil servants have been accused of manipulating delays in order to scupper freedom of information.The startling revelations about MPs' expenses would not have been available to the Daily Telegraph if the Parliamentary authorities had not been preparing a heavily censored document for FOI release - five years after the information was first requested.

Christopher Graham, the new Commissioner for Information, is a former producer for Radio 4's investigative programme File on Four and is committed to tackling the backlog of cases. One indication he is succeeding is that the number of decision notices issued in 2009 was up 40 per cent on the year before.

Graham has warned the 100,000 public bodies in the UK covered by the Act that: "We are now in a freedom of information age. Public organisations have to put a good case to withhold information, or it will be released.

"When the message gets through that we will be coming after them, things will speed up and there will be less gamesmanship."

Freedom of Information

The Freedom of Information Act, which came into force at the beginning of 2005, gives individuals or organisations the right to request information held by a public authority.

The public authority must tell the applicant whether it holds the information, and must normally supply it within 20 working days.

Some information is exempted by the Act and the public authority does not have to confirm or deny the existence of the information or provide it if an exemption applies.

Some exemptions, like national security, are absolute. Others are qualified, which means that the public authority must decide whether the public interest in using the exemption outweighs the public interest in releasing the information.

If an applicant is unhappy with a refusal to disclose information, they can complain to the Information Commissioner's Office which will either uphold the authority's use of an exemption or decide that the information must be disclosed.

The Act is fully retrospective and applies to all information, not just information filed since it came into force.

The scope of the Act:

It covers recorded information held by public authorities in England, Northern Ireland and Wales. Public authorities include:

- Central government and government departments
- Local authorities
- Hospitals, doctors' surgeries, dentists, pharmacists and opticians
- State schools, colleges and universities
- Police forces and prison services

Exemptions and how they work

There are 23 exemptions in the Act. Some of them are 'absolute' and relate, for example, to information concerning to bodies like the security service (MI5) and the secret intelligence service (MI6). Most of the exemptions, however, are termed 'qualified', If a public authority believes that the information is covered by a qualified exemption it must apply the public interest test.

The public interest test favours disclosure where a qualified exemption or an exception applies. In such cases, the information may be withheld only if the public authority considers that the public interest in withholding the information is greater than the public interest in disclosing it.

A full list of exemptions to the Act, either absolute or qualified, is kept up to date by the Information Commissioners Office and can be accessed via:

http://www.ico.gov.uk/home/what_we_cover/freedom_of_information/guidance.aspx#exeguidance

How to make a request.

Contact the public authority directly. All freedom of information requests must be in writing (this includes email) and must provide the applicant's name and an address for a response.

*There is no need to say you are asking for information under the Freedom of Information Act but mentioning it can help.

* Describe the information as clearly as possible – if your request is too broad or unclear the public authority may ask you to be more specific and this will cause delay.

* You can express a reasonable preference for the format you wish the information to be supplied in, for example, by email or as a paper copy.

What happens once the request has been received?

Public authorities must respond promptly to requests or, in any event, within 20 working days although under freedom of information they have longer to consider whether the disclosure of normally exempt information would be in the public interest. When considering the public interest test, the public authority must do so 'within a reasonable time'.

What if the information is refused?

When a public authority decides not to disclose the information it must give its reasons. It must explain how the exemption or exception applies and it must explain the arguments under the public interest test. The role of the Information Commissioner's Office (ICO) is to enforce and promote the Act. It has responsibility for ensuring that information is disclosed promptly and that exemptions from disclosure are applied lawfully.

The legal process?

You may apply to the ICO for a decision about whether the request has been dealt with according to the Act if, for example, you believe there has been excessive delay or if you wish to dispute the application of an exemption or refusals made on public interest grounds.

The ICO may serve a decision notice on the public authority either confirming the decision made by the public authority or directing it to disclose information within a certain time. Non-compliance with a decision notice may constitute contempt of court.

If you or the public authority disagrees with the ICO's decision you have 28 days to appeal to the Independent Information Tribunal. The Information Tribunal may uphold the ICO's decision notice, amend it (for example change the time frame for release of information) or overturn it. Non-compliance with the Information Tribunal's notice may also constitute contempt of court.

Environmental Information Regulations

The Environmental Information Regulations give members of the public the right to access environmental information held by public authorities. The request can be made by letter, email, telephone or in person.

The regulations apply to most public authorities, but they can also apply to any organisation or person carrying out a public administration function and any organisation or person under the control of a public authority which has environmental responsibilities.

This can include private companies or public private partnerships such as companies involved in energy, water, waste and transport.

Environmental information is divided into six main areas:
* The state of the elements of the environment, such as air, water, land, animals.
* Emissions and discharges, noise, energy, radiation, waste.
* Policies and activities likely to affect elements of the environment.
* Economic reports and analyses.
* Human health and safety and contamination of the food chain.
* Cultural sites, structures, to the extent they may be affected by the environment.

If a public authority receives a request for information on any of these areas they are legally obliged to provide it, usually within 20 working days.

There are a number of exceptions to this rule and, if this is the case, the public authority must explain why the exception applies. The exceptions include:
* The information is personal to someone else and it wouldn't be fair to release it;
* Disclosing the information would put national security at risk; or
* The information is confidential and commercially sensitive.

In almost all cases, the authority must also consider whether the public interest in keeping the information secret outweighs the public interest in making it available.

Making a request for information
People have a legal right to request any recorded information held by a public authority and do not have to know whether the information is environmental – it is for the authority to work this out. The relevant authority must be contacted direct. There are no restrictions on how the request is made but it is best to make it in writing. The authority must reply in writing. Every public authority must have a complaints procedure relating to the EIR. If the authority refuses a request for information, it must tell the inquirer how to complain.

The authority should deal with the complaint within 40 working days. It must state whether it accepts that the request was handled wrongly, and if so what it will do to put this right. If that is not satisfactory a complaint can be made to the Information Commissioner.

COPYRIGHT

It is one of the most readily understood symbols in the world - and it is not really needed.

The idea that you must mark your work with the symbol to establish copyright is a misconception. Copyright comes into action automatically as soon as a work is created and it gives the copyright holder the right to sue anyone who uses the work without permission.

All the holder has to do is satisfy the test of originality, that the work is the product of the holder's skill, creativity or time.

Copyright protects any literary, artistic, or musical work, sound recordings, films, broadcasts, pictures and graphics. The layout and the content of newspapers and magazines is also protected as is material published on the internet.

BUT

There is no copyright in facts, news, information or ideas expressed verbally.

AND

Parts of copyright works can be reproduced by the media in the course of reporting current events or for the purposes of criticism or review, although this "fair dealing" concession does not extend to photographs of current events.

REMEDIES FOR BREACH OF COPYRIGHT

The copyright owner can apply for an injunction in the county court or the High Court to restrain any infringement of his copyright. He can also claim damages and obtain an order for the possession of offending copies of the material.

Copyright in general

Copyright issues are governed by Copyright, Designs and Patents Act 1988. The Act gives protection to three categories of original work

1. Literary, dramatic, musical or artistic works

Literary covers books, newspaper comment, features and stories, interviews and reports of speeches - anything written down, anywhere.
Artistic covers pictures, graphics and all types of art work.

2. Sound recordings, films or broadcasts

Sound recordings cover any recording of sound regardless of how made.
Film covers recording of a moving image.
Broadcast covers the electronic transmission of images, sounds and information to the public - it does not include the internet unless it is a live event transmitted on the net at the same time as it is being broadcast.

3. Typographical arrangements of published editions

Typographical arrangements cover the way a printed page is designed and also protects against unauthorised photo-copying.

The test to establish copyright is simple: All that is needed is proof that the work is original and the product of one's own skill and labour and has not been copied from some other body of work. It does not need to be of any high literary standard nor to be strikingly original.

Length of copyright

The following applies only to work created after the Copyright, Designs and Patents Act came into effect on July 31, 1989.

* Literary, dramatic, musical and artistic works - 70 years from the end of the year in which the creator of the work dies.

* Sound recordings - 50 years from the end of the year in which they were made.

* Broadcasts - 50 years from the end of the year in which they were made.

* Typographical arrangements - 25 years from the end of the year in which first published.

* Films - 70 years from the end of the year in which the last among the director, screen writer or music composer died.

Ownership of copyright

COMMERCIAL RIGHTS

The first owner of the copyright is the author except when the work has been done in the course of employment. Then the employer becomes the copyright holder, unless there is an agreement to the contrary. This means that articles written by staff writers or pictures taken by staff photographers can be sold by the employer to whom he pleases.

The case is different with freelances. The key date is July 31, 1989, the day the Copyright Act went in to force. Freelance articles or pictures commissioned by a newspaper before 31.7.89 belong to the newspaper. After 31.7.89 the copyright has been retained by the freelance writer or freelance photographer.

The publisher has no automatic right to copyright of work done by freelances even if the work was ordered. If the publisher wishes to acquire the copyright it has to be via a written assignment by the copyright holder and signed by him.

The copyright holder can license the publisher to use his work but if it is an exclusive licence this must also be in writing.

MORAL RIGHTS 1.

The author of copyright work in general also has moral rights as follows:

1. The right to be identified as the author.

2. The rght not to have his work subjected to derogatory treatment.

3. The right not to have work falsely attributed to him.

BUT the right (1) to be identified and (2) not to have his work subjected to derogatory treatment does not apply to work created for publication in a newspaper, magazine or periodical nor to any work made available for such publication with the consent of the author. For the media this means the work can be subjected to the ruthless attention of the sub-editors.

The right (3) not to have work falsely attributed to a person **does** apply to newspapers, magazines or periodicals. If a famous person, for instance, gives no more than an interview to a newspaper and the paper publishes an article purporting to have been actually written by the person himself, he may have an action for false attribution.

MORAL RIGHTS 2.

Person who commissions a picture

Anyone who commissions a picture for *private and domestic purposes* is protected by the moral right not to have copies of the picture issued to the public even if he does not own the commercial copyright.

Let us say there has been a family occasion – a wedding – and the groom commissions a commercial photographer to cover the celebrations. Years later the groom is in the news and a relative supplies the media with a copy of a picture of the groom and his bride on their wedding day.

If the original photograph was taken before 31.7.89 the commercial copyright belongs to the person who commissioned the picture – the bridegroom.

If taken after 31.7.89 the commercial copyright belongs to the person who takes the picture – the photographer, unless there is an agreement to the contrary.

But the groom has another right – the moral right not to have copies of the picture issued to the public.

The relative who lends the picture is unlikely to own the copyright (unless he took it).

Therefore, if the media used the picture, two rights may have been infringed.

1. The commercial copyright which belongs (after 31.7.89) to the photographer.

2. The moral right not to have it made public - which belongs to the bridegroom.

Copyright in speeches

Copyright attaches to spoken words as soon as they are recorded in a permanent form, with or without the permission of the speaker. But it is not an infringement of the speaker's copyright to use the words for reporting current events as long as, broadly:

 1. The speaker did not prohibit the recording of his words.
 2. The use made of the words was not of a kind prohibited by the speaker or copyright owner BEFORE the speech was made.

 * There is no copyright in the FACTS conveyed in the speaker's words.

 * A secret recording of the speaker's words is not a breach of copyright.

 * There is copyright in the manuscript from which the speaker reads.

For example: In December 1992 The Sun was sent an advance copy of the Queen's Christmas Day message which was embargoed until after it had been broadcast. The owner of the copyright of embargoed material has the right to enforce terms for its use and can take action if those terms are breached. The Sun published the message two days before the broadcast under the headline " OUR DIFFICULT DAYS, by the Queen" and was forced to pay damages to charity for breach of copyright.

CROWN COPYRIGHT

Work created by civil servants in the course of their work is protected by Crown Copyright. Pictures of the wedding of Charles Bronson "Britain's most dangerous man", taken by a prison warder using a prison camera were deemed by the High Court to be Crown Copyright and Mrs Bronson was forbidden to use the pictures in her autobiography after the Prison Service claimed people were trying to cash in on the "Bronson Cult".

INTERNET COPYRIGHT

As far as infringements of copyright are concerned the law of the nation where the infringement took place applies. For journalists in the United Kingdom this means the 1998 Act. It is not so much where the copyright work was created as where it was downloaded and used without permission.

Most countries are signatories to the Berne Convention on copyright and the Universal Copyright Convention. This provides reciprocal protection of copyright around the world. It is illegal to copy material into the United Kingdom which, if you had made a copy of it in the UK, would have been an infringement of copyright.

It would be illegal to link and pass off the content as your own. It would be best to seek permission from the webmaster of the proposed link. The best practice is to link to the Home page of the site so that the information on the site is not presented out of context although most media sources have clear identity markers on every page.

Infringements of copyright

If the owner of the copyright considers that his work has been used in a way that has been unfair to him he must show that copying has taken place and that a 'substantial' part had been copied. There is no percentage figure of what constitutes a 'substantial' part.

Example (Actual): Journalist Julie Burchill took a tiny percentage, just 200 or 300 words, from a 300-page biography to complete a profile she was writing but they were the 'juicy bits', interviews with school friends of the subject which the interviewer had created by her skill and labour. Burchill was found to have infringed the copyright.

Example (Hypothetical): A group picture of the Michael Douglas - Zeta Jones wedding is cropped so that all the guests are discarded and all that remains are Douglas and Zeta Jones. Isolating that newsworthy part of the picture, even though it may have been, say, just 10pc of the area of the whole picture, would count as 'substantial'.

POINTS

Lifting stories: There is no copyright in facts but persistent lifting of facts from another media, even if the stories are rewritten each time, may still be an infringement because of the skill, labour and judgment that went into the researching of the stories. In the early days of local radio, for example, when some stations were starting on a shoestring, it was noticeable that the content of their news bulletins improved dramatically after the first edition of the local evening paper landed at the station.

Outside contributors: The copyright of work submitted by outside contributors (unpaid or paid) will normally be held by the contributor who can withdraw the facility and impose charges as he wishes. There are numerous examples ranging from reports of amateur sports to syndicated TV and radio programming.

Readers Letters: There is an implicit licence from the writer to use this copyright material freely for one occasion but the copyright is still retained by the author. The same principle would not apply to a freelance journalist whose work was used without any prior negotiation over a fee.

Screen Grabs: Publication, without permission, of the whole or a substantial part of a TV image is an infringement of copyright.

Defences to breach of copyright

FAIR DEALING

The concept of Fair Dealing gives the media the opportunity to use a fair portion of copyright work provided there is:

* Sufficient acknowledgement of the work from which it is taken.
* Acknowledgement of the author of the work.

There is no need to approach the copyright holder in advance but Fair Dealing is restricted to two specific areas:

* Current events. Note that pictures are *excluded* from this area of Fair Dealing.
* Criticism or review. Pictures are *included* and can be used in Fair Dealing.

An important proviso is that - when used for the purposes of criticism or review - the work has been lawfully made available to the public, which rules out confidential material such as private letters. One of the tests by which the law measures whether the copyright infringement constitutes fair dealing is the degree to which the use competes with that of the copyright holder.

If, for example, David Beckham published a book which contained a large number of exclusive pictures. Had a newspaper reprinted 20 of the pictures on the pretext of reviewing the book this would probably hit sales of the book and would not be fair dealing. If one picture, maybe two, were used this might be fair dealing - but, if one of the pictures was the most sensational ever taken of Beckham and was a major part of the book's attraction, it might not be fair dealing.

PUBLIC INTEREST

The 1988 Act recognises the common law defence of public interest against any action for breach of copyright. The Court of Appeal has said that there is a defence of public interest to actions in both copyright and confidentiality if it could be shown there was a public interest to publish the picture. For example, the defence would kick in if you obained a classified Ministry of Defence picture which shows troops undergoing chemical warfare tests in inadequate equipment and the Ministry claimed copyright in an attempt to stop you using the picture.

ACQUIESCENCE

If the owner of copyright material has previously encouraged or allowed another to make use of that material without complaint or any action to stop it, this might destroy a later claim for infringement of copyright